The Jews & The Blues

Father Mothers Creation Through Israel

DeDe & Pelham Gross

Foreword: Daniel Gray,
Trail-buddy on this less traveled highway

Blues: Dan Gray & Tim Gross

Includes Ann Schrader: "In a Trance with the God
of the Jews"

XULON PRESS

Emphasis and parentheses within Scripture passages are the author's. **Bold** print elsewhere in the text is the author's.

Spelling: Blues is informal, loose, and free-flowing. So is some of the spelling.

Xulon Press
10640 Main Street
Suite 204
Fairfax, VA 22030
(703) 934-4411
XulonPress.com

To order additional copies, call 1-866-909-BOOK (2665).

Dedication

———◦———

Here's how the man saw it. He called himself "Daniel's He-Goat"—the male goat coming out of the west, riding on the wind to smash the ram of dead religion and destroy both its horns—Catholic and Protestant dead-religion prisons. The goat pulverized the carcass, then was pictured as standing over the ram's remains, "watering them down" (let the reader understand), and walking away in victory to build the **real,** non-religious, kingdom of God. He was a fierce, heaven fired from the bone out pioneer—a true John the Baptist forerunner.

He said he was stepping into the role of "The manchild" (See Rev 12 KJV). He preached it, he sang it: "I'm the manchild of God, spoken of in his word—made so by the grace of Jesus, my Lord." (Meaning the resurrected fiery Christ was burning in the earth in his own human flesh, blood and life. You think **this** didn't cause a furor! He was caught up in

v

God while still blazing a trail through the jungled-down, religious wilderness of the seventies, with his "Elijah's mantle" falling back into the earth (though we buried his body) for whosoever to pick it up.

For me he was the scapegoat of God in human flesh, sent into the dark desert of my life to blaze me into the living Way. He was my sacrifice "caught in the bushes" on the mountain of God. He laid the foundation, the **living** Christ, in my life, and seeded all the revelations that grow in me.

He went down (to be caught up) in 1975—still swinging, axe in hand—still cutting, sword in mouth—still burning, fire in soul—still charging, reckless in faith 'til he died on down and went on up. God used his death like a streaking star across the darkened heavenlies to light my way. When everyone else gave up on getting me freed up from seminary ingrained, embedded, false theology, he stuck with me and became my spiritual father. Just before he crossed over, he spiritually "gutted" me publicly and spoke into me, he said, "the guts of Christ." The following is part of the apostolic charge he gave me:

"God had pointed his finger at him and said to me, 'I **want** him. You shall suffer and you shall **get** him.' I said, 'He's **yours**—so help me God!' The word of God is like a hammer. It strikes and breaks and penetrates. It's the **living** Word. I said, 'Father, hath been given me the words of fire to **burn** that false theological doctrine of Satan out of his mind, and **burn** in the truth of the living God.' So I held him through Christ by the gift of faith and I **smashed** him, and I **smashed** him with **fire** of God and judgment—word after word, line upon line, great hollering, great destruction by the word of God. By the power of God I have now **smashed** this theological mind to bits and delivered a great mind, **the mind of Christ**, filled with the Bible, the Book of Life—delivered it unto life, now ready to minister its life and doctrine, power and dominion, and bring forth God's fullness in his people."

Well, Brother Pruett, sad to say: some of that jungle junk got me all tangled again, but, like you said and showed, God was faithful. He freed me to fight on another day. Twenty seven years down the road, I'm still "bull-dogging" ahead like you told me I would **have** to do. Remember? Standing outside your Country Air place about two in the morning? It's my **great** honor, privilege, and pleasure to dedicate this book to you, "Papa Pruett":

J. W. Pruett, Senior—
"He being dead still speaks"

Thanks Gang!

━━━━▶▶◦◦◀◀━━━━

Who touched me? All who have touched my life over the years have a part in this book. Some touched to soften my heart, others to sharpen my sword—some thought to do one and ended up doing the other. No matter—God used you to grow me. I pray he uses me now to bless you.

Special favors for these—Lord, if you please:
To my creative, enthusiastic, Song of Solomon "DeDe"—God-sent to be my wife, June 16, 2002, and to her sons: Mark, Todd, David, and their families for trusting me "going away with Mama." Love to all of you. Thanks "DeDe Girl" for: loving me to keep on living, keep on going, keep on writing—for your complete understanding, enduring devotion, and ever-ready, cheerful kindness, for loving what God gives me to write, and for faithfully poring over the manuscript with me. Oh—You! Your prayers, your

servant's heart! A definite **wow!** Take a bow. You took my heart, "Shugah." You are truly an *eshet-chayil* ('a capable wife,' Proverbs 31:10-31) and an *ezer k'negdi* ("a companion suitable for helping me," Genesis 2:18). (Borrowed from David Stern [about his wife], page 1v, Complete Jewish Bible)

To my children and their families—Deborah, Timothy, Phyllis, and Shane—my "grands" and all my downline—always suffering with me—and sometimes too much without me—while God was working me over, and working this out in me. **Thank you. Love you all!**

To all my spiritual children—all who call me "papa," including (but not limited to) Victory, David, Jessica; Mary Carmen, Javier, Alma Rosa and all their families

To Daniel Gray, faithful trail buddy—always hunting Elijah's Highway with me. Thanks for pulling me out of the pasture and taking me "on the road again"—and for letting me use your Blues stuff! Love you, brother! Hope this flickers a "Highway Up Ahead" light for you.

To Peter Loth, Valerie, and family for being our encourager-friends. Pete is a Jew, one of only about 5,000 Holocaust survivors left. He said, **"Don't back down. Print the book!"** Here it is, Pete. May it make a difference for your people—and mine. Love you guys.

To my "long-haulers"—James and Rhea Ratliff ("Pa and Ma"), James and Shirley Madearis, Geneva, Tim, and Shane who listened over the years, across thousands of miles, to what God was giving me—and **rescued me** more'n once from "demon jaws and dragon claws." God bless you so that you have to "lay down with it!"

To Pastors Tom and Rose Hayden and "The Seeds of Faith" who kept on—and keep on—loving and encouraging me to keep on being "papa." Rose, you'll always be resident "editor-in-heart!" Thanks, love to you all.

To Pastors Alan and Carol Koch for standing in the gap—through all the rap—so the free presence of God can swallow me up afresh and anew to renew and renew!

To Pastors Jim and Elizabeth Maher, our new congregational pastors in Forerunner Christian Fellowship. We support you in carrying out "God's Mandate for Israel."

To Messianic Jewish Rabbi Jerry Feldman, whose passionate, wisdom-loaded, truth kindness arrested me and stoked my furnace with Yeshua—Messiah of Israel, King of the Jews! Love appreciation to you, my brother!

To Pastors Steve and Kathy Gray and all the "Smithton Outpourers"—Thanks for pouring love and truth into my life from 1998-2002, four wonder-filled years. Blessings from here to glory—and all in it! Let's let love keep on pressing—to give out the blessing.

To Mike, Diane Bickle and family, who lashed themselves to the mast and keep hanging onto God through all kinds of storms to launch and lead Shiloh Estates—"Friends of the Bridegroom (FOTB)," "International House of Prayer Kansas City

(IHOP)," Forerunner School of Prayer (FSOP), Forerunner Christian Fellowship (FCF), and other ministries. The presence of God during the fifty days of extravagant worship provided the delivery room for "The Jews & The Blues." **Love all you lovers, worshippers, and "pray-ers."**

To Mark Murphree, FSOP's Heart and Pen teacher, and all my classmates—Thanks, with love, for sharing your lives and gifts. Critique the book—and write a better one!

To all my "old" midnight-daylight running buddies, who rode out that **extra** mile to bring revival in the land—to Blues-man Dan, Shelley Gee; Shelley Dee and Brice; Scotty, Ann, and Anna; Arnold, "Firecracker" Shannon, and "Court"; Joe; Mike, Brenda, Jimmy and Matt; George and Nola; John and Thora; James and Shirley; Mike, Regina, and Jessica; Dr. Al, Janna, Erin, and Chris; Cheryl; Paula; Bill, Karen and Will; Nancy; Susie; Tara; "Missy"; Scott and Mel; Deb; John and Heather; Sue and Rita; Roger and Carol; Leroy and Darlene; Jo-El; Steve and Missy; Jason; Angelica and Vandi; Tim, Kim, Travis, Rachel, Ben, Joel, Aaron, and Josh; Lesley, Joel, Kevin, and Corey; Mary, Sarah, Erin; "California Mary," Mia, Shay, Carrie, Kerri, Traci, (other) Carrie, Randy, Sherry, Shannon and Robby; Scott, Lisa and Jesse; Hollie, Arne, "Big Dan"; Cliff, Julie, and Jeana; Billy, Michelle, Geneva, Michael and Gail, Mike and Shirley, Kuda, Nancy, Charra, and **all you other** Light Riders who saddled up with "The Posse" against darkness. Thanks for letting me be the "road dog papa." **You**

brought healing to my heart and hope to my soul!
(If I missed a name, call Shannon!)

   **To those in all the churches who welcomed
"The Posse"**—churches with pastors like Dick and
Lisa, Randy and Tina, Allen and Linda, Mark and
Mary, Ken and Karen, Todd and Dorrie, Patty, Barry
and Claire, Paul and Jan, Tom and Ginger, Damon,
Steve, and others. Love you!

Contents

———➤•◄———

Contents

Foreword

Funny how it works. You think you have all your ducks in a row—all the answers, all your religious "preferences" stacked up and sorted neatly—like spices in a rack. That **is** what most Christians want, you know—resolution, closure on the matter. "God said it, I believe it, that settles it" is a nice statement of faith, but, unfortunately, most of us have settled a few matters nicely and then stopped listening. True faith, however, rarely leaves us settled, but tends to keep us on a journey as it did Abraham, the friend of God and the father of faith-walkers. These faith-walkers are forever looking outward on the horizon, up at the stars, or forward to the promise, but **rarely** are they settled in to comfort. I'm afraid many of us resemble Lot, who moved into town with his family, much more than we do Abraham.

So it was that I found myself in my comfortable

country home where I had raised my sons and rebuilt my life out of the ashes, thinking all was fine now, all was orderly, when the call came to tell me about a little girl I barely knew—the daughter of some dear pastor friends. The call was to tell me she had a tumor in her brain. What occurred in my life that day and the days that followed turned the tables over again and, suddenly, my heart was on the move again—to find answers, to find more. Nothing in my life has been the same since. (See "Author's Tribute" following this.)

From the three days of intercession that followed—the groanings inside me, groanings too deep to utter or even understand—did not come answers, but a whole new set of questions with one general guideline. Over time we began calling the guideline "Get the Picture", which essentially says that the pictures and types in the Bible are not there to be looked at like artwork but to be used as maps or blueprints or instructions. It wasn't long before everything in my life, ministry, and Christian walk was seen through get-the-picture glasses. If Enoch and Elijah are anything, they are pictures of what it can be like for us on the highway through the desert. (Next time you wanna figure out who's gonna—and who's not gonna—"rapture," try using the pictures as your examples instead of your nice, neat religion.)

So it is with Israel and modern Gentile Christianity: we have it all figured out and neatly arranged—or at least put out of sight where we don't have to think about it. No big deal to **us** that we're holding fast to the very ideas that eventually led to

The Holocaust, as long as we don't have to fool with it. We might be one who is a "replacement" type, or one who is fascinated by Jewish stuff, or one who believes Jesus is a blond-haired, blue eyed Jew from a lost tribe (a contradiction in terms), but our life doesn't have time for Israel right now. Too bad. Without it, without **her**, we cannot complete the picture and become the glorious church.

Wanna picture? Let's say we're baking a cake. We need ingredients. We survey our kitchen and find everything we need except eggs. We can't make our cake—we can **try,** but no one will want to eat whatever we come up with. Our priority then must be to get eggs, to get our missing ingredient. **Then,** we can bake our cake.

Much like the good shepherd who leaves the found to go after that which is lost, we, as Christians, need to leave our nicely arranged religion rack and go out and find the thing we're missing—the missing eggs (be sure to get a full dozen)—and **then** get to baking, realizing of course that the end product isn't an omelet, but a new creation wherein the eggs and all the other ingredients will blend together till separation becomes impossible.

Pelham Gross, "Papa" as he's known to many of us unorthodox table-turners, will take you on a journey full of twists and turns like nothing you've ever read. It'll be much like a roller coaster and you'll have to hang on at times, but if you can just "get the picture," perhaps you'll have a paradigm shift of your own and join us, the crazy Christians, who don't know where they're going or how to get there—only that we're headed home to the promised land, and if we stay on the highway and stay in motion, we may not ever get the feeling of having a place to lay our head in this world, but we can look forward to home in Jerusalem. So hang on, and let Papa drive for a while. It may be a wild ride—things may topple and fall, and the neatness of your life may be disrupted—some things may go out the window, but if we keep heading down the highway we may yet get home.

Daniel Gray

(Author's note: Look for nobody-does-Blues-like Dan's upcoming Lamentations CD.)

Author's Tribute: For The Love of Hannah

Tragedy! Seemed like it, felt like it, had every outward mark of it. **God** turned it around and used it as a catapult trigger-release for Dan, myself, and others. It was August 20, 2001—we buried Hannah in a wedding dress—at her request. She was twelve—said she was marrying Jesus. What do you do? What do you say? She was loving, trusting— daughter of faithful, pioneering revival pastors, Dick and Lisa Drummeller of Crystalbrook Church, Liberty, Kansas.

When doctors said "terminal" eighteen months earlier, word went out over the revival circuit, and many began praying earnestly with fasting. Among these, Care Pastor Daniel Gray of The Smithton

Outpouring—family friend, revival preacher at Crystalbrook Church several times. Hannah's terminal diagnosis knocked him into the deepest, groaning intercession of his life. Immediately, he began crying out to God—shut away and on his face for 3 days, no food. For a year and a half he racked up the hours and miles from KC to Liberty to visit and minister to Hannah and her family. His bonding with Hannah in the Spirit put him into a new intercession realm. Out of that was born the last sermon in Smithton in the Smithton Outpouring. Dan preached it: "Get The Picture."

Fresh truth stirred the Spirit of revelation in me. Dan and I set out together to find "Elijah's Highway" (that caught-up-with-God place of intimate power), not just for ourselves, but for the bride that Hannah is such a deep part of. "Jews & Blues" has these Hannah beginnings; thanks "mother" Hannah. We love you! We're turning tragedy into triumph, trumpeting Truth about your Jesus-Husband—all along this road less traveled. Keep traveling with us in the Spirit realm—you and the bride. We're determined—by the grace of God.

If "Jews & Blues" was born of tragedy, it was conceived in the pain fields of wrecked cars and lives; wrecked churches and marriages; wrecked faith and finances; and wrecked feelings in every direction. Not a lot unlike Israel's history. Can you identify with any of this?

Introduction:
Taking Aim

In the foreword, Dan was baking a cake and needed eggs—a full dozen, all 12 tribes, the full nation of Israel—to bake the Gentile Church "cake" into a glorious church. Let's take it one level further. Question: what do we do with the cake the Gentiles bake? Give it to God? Good idea—but **where**? **Where** do we "meet God" to give it to him? Of course he's already "in the mix," in the "cake"— suffering in the making and the glory-fire baking— but where does **God** want it offered to him for his glory? "The Jews & The Blues" says, "One place— and **one place only—in the nation of Israel.** Abba will receive it **only** in the capitol city of Jerusalem, Israel. **That's** what sets this book apart (and maybe a few years ahead, but I couldn't wait). God's plan, in the final stages, is **not** for Gentiles to receive Jews into "the church." Rather, in these **final** stages, God's plan **requires** Gentiles to become part of God's heart for Israel. From **that nation** God harvests all the nations, sets up his everlasting kingdom in earth, and rules his creation.

So the person who won't holler, **"Whoa!"**—then scream, one way or another, at this generation's status quo will never get you where you want to go. Traditions of Father Abraham, Isaac, Israel, and others are one thing, but **present** day traditions? Oh boy! **Quite** another story. "Jews & Blues" is **deliberately** calculated to **make** you rethink:

- ❏ Israel's Destiny as a Nation—God's wife in earth.
- ❏ Kingdom of God—Do Jews need to get in the church? Or the church into Israel?
- ❏ Replacement Theology—Conceived in confusion, born in Babylon.
- ❏ God and Gender—Is God really100 percent male?
- ❏ "Good ol' Boys" Church Club—Too many women molested at the church "male-box."
- ❏ Women—Expressing God's female side.
- ❏ Blues—They got saved!
- ❏ Rapture, Second Coming, Millennialism— Not **"left behind,"** leaving **early!**
- ❏ Church Empires, Mega Churches—**Whose** "kingdom" is it? **Really?**
- ❏ Kingdom mysteries—Fullness of Gentiles, two olive trees, women in The Revelation.

Women and Jews are, today, still singing the Blues. What I'm **aiming** to show is (1) Israel's usefulness, (2) God's femaleness, and (3) how these two are interrelated—intertwined, interwoven into God's fabric. Do I hit where I'm aiming? You get to make the call.

(1) Israel's usefulness: No way—absolutely **no way** is God done using Israel as a **nation.** I'm not talking about Israel as a spiritual entity of spooky dimensions. I mean, a nation in the sense that America is a nation. That "the church replaced Israel" (Replacement Theology) is ridiculous in light of the Scriptures. The church is not a nation. God has not and will not drop Israel as a nation and make one out of the church—**never** says he will. He chose Israel, he judged Israel, he loves Israel, and he's sticking with her—forever.

(2) God's femaleness: Men can carry God's authority with love—we'd better—but the church club of the "Good old boys?" **That wall has to fall.** Reason? God's no longer going to hide—that he's got a "female side." He's revealing this feminine side now from the Scriptures to bust some **church-house** locks for women to **hurry up** into God-given destinies. He wants them freed up to do their destinies—either **with** God-obeying husbands—or **without** 'em. Having a husband can be a wonderful part of God's big-picture plan, but it's **not required** for a woman to become totally absorbed into the "female side" of God, and in this oneness through Jesus, receive **full satisfaction of reward.** Yes, a husband **can be** wonderful, but who do I have to tell? A husband can be hell—and hold a woman's soul in the bottom of a hole—all in the name of God.

(Maybe holding a Bible and hollering, "**Submit!**")

(3) The Interrelationship: You'll find this challenging, and you'll just have to trust me a little at this point when I say, "It **is** rewarding." It's really simple—once you've read the book by the Spirit, but I'm telling you up-front, it con-fronts old paradigms. What else can I say? I think this is part of that "paradigm shift" you're hearing about. Obviously, I believe it's God out-front. I won't guarantee that you'll "get it all" the first time through. **I** didn't when God gave it to me. I've been busy listening, writing, and **experiencing** some of this for **decades**. The "Jews and Israel" encounter I had was the "last piece of the puzzle" to fall in place. It rose up to be the centerpiece and plumb-bob in the big-God-picture before me and in me. So, as "Pa" used to say (and I think big Papa is saying it now), "Take your time with this—and hurry up every chance you get—I need it done **yesterday**! " Be Spirit led, Spirit fed, and Spirit overrun. Living in the **overflow** is "where it's at."

I see an interwoven working of God's inner-self workings—Alpha-Omega workings. Alpha is the beginning; Omega the ending, but Omega can roll right back into Alpha in that realm apart from time. God is both—and all in between. He can finish what he began; he can begin where he just finished—Omega looping right back into Alpha and coming all over again. God's eternal; he's **big**. When Yeshua (Jesus) took his blood into Father God's Holy Heart, a glorification took place and a mature, completely obedient-to-God specimen of humanity was love-absorbed into the Godhead. God "married" humanity in a first-forerunner way to form a Divine Creature that **never before existed**. As heaven adjusted to this additional Godhead fullness, the "new heavens" that Isaiah, Peter, and John saw was created. (Isa 65:17, 66:22, 2 Pet 3:13, Rev 21:1) God began immediately to make this powerful, new God-Creature known in earth by appearing in earth—one such appearance being to John on the Isle of Patmos (Rev 1:10-20). From those appearances, God began a fresh working to create the new earth to match the new heavens. This is a work in progress today as people call on the Name of the Lord, and this God-Creature—Yeshua, Abba, Spirit—merges into their lives—God-Spirit into human-spirit. (More details on this in the Glossary under "3-thru." You really need those details to understand the book, **but**, you also need to get the piece by piece understanding of the book to understand the details. Just know details are there—and be Spirit led. That's about the best I can tell you.)

Each chapter will stand-alone, with the more closely related chapters being grouped as best we could manage. I have **no** doubt you'll be refreshed as you're being challenged. But, in all fairness, I should remind you of the old proverb about the fire and the kitchen. What is it? "If you can't stand the fire, stay outta the kitchen?" Something like that! You won't catch me beating around the bush, but I **don't** beat on you—not intentionally. If it seems I do, give me some grace—I'm really **aiming** at your **enemy.** He could be hiding from **you** like he was from **me.** (I think he's the same enemy.) I'm shooting at old jail-house thought systems in your head. If you're not breathing a little freer when you finish the book, forgive me for failing. Whoever you are, wherever you're reading this—I'm **for** you; I really am. Let's get geared up together, let heaven's love harness us to glorify Jesus Christ, and give our Daddy back his wife in his dream-garden.

My wife tells this true-life experience. Her family had a little A-framed cabin in the woods across the river from Washington, Missouri. On one of their family outings, DeDe was standing beside the raised deck. Son Mark, about 3 at the time, pointed across to something at his eye-level. DeDe's dad, an avid target shooter, was nearby with his rifle. His sharp eye followed Mark's finger. **"Don't move!"** he yelled, and pointed the rifle at DeDe. She froze in trusting obedience. **"Kapow!"** Her dad then came and removed, from right where DeDe was standing, the poisonous, but now **headless**, copperhead snake from a deck post. When people you love are in danger, you'll run a risk to rescue 'em.

Part One:
The Jews

CHAPTER 1

Jesus and Jerry Going After Haman

————▷•◦•◁————

Haman The Invader

It was after someone identified to me the violence against the Jews down through the generations (The Crusades, The Holocaust, etc.) **to the present day**, as being fueled by the "spirit of Haman" that I understood a dream I had late in 2001. It was heart-hurting vivid—left me **sick**—**so** sick I meant to forget it—told only one person. She insisted I write it down, but I resisted—did **not** want to **do** that. It shocked my memory with repulsive waves. It **hurt** so I put it off.—didn't do it. ('Think you'll soon understand why.) But God was determined to get my attention on Jews and Israel so he must have said, "If it takes a horrendous dream to get the boy's attention, **well then."**

First, a little review on Haman and what he was

about: (See Esther 3) "[4]Day after day they spoke to him (Mordecai) but he refused to comply. Therefore they told Haman about it to see whether Mordecai's behavior would be tolerated, **for he had told them he was a Jew. . . . Haman looked for a way to destroy all Mordecai's people, the Jews. . . .** [13]Dispatches were sent by couriers to all the king's provinces with the order to destroy, **kill and annihilate all the Jews—young and old, women and little children—on a single day. . . . The king and Haman sat down to drink,** but the city. . . was bewildered."

Now, here's my dream that I tried to delete. None of the characters were identified in the dream, but now I understand the central figure to be the spirit of Haman. I witnessed and sensed entities acting in a darkened environment. I saw forms or outlines of beings, frantically darting in and out of the shadows, bowing and catering to Haman, who was obviously distressed to the max. He made demands in angry tones, as beings all about him bowed and brought him what they thought would appease him. Haman refused all offers, one after another, with growing displeasure. The terror level rose in the other beings in proportion to Haman's anger.

Nothing they did or offered satisfied Haman. Suddenly, Haman lost control. Like a two year old brat gripped in a temper tantrum, he started screaming, kicking, and went into an uncontrollable rage. I was riveted on Haman. He wheeled, first one way, then another, as he struck out at those doing their utmost to serve and please him. I watched as rage threw him down. He writhed as his wild, piercing shriek hit the rest of the beings: "No! No! No! I want more Jews! Bring me more Jews! More Jews! **Cook me some more Jews!**"

I woke up Jew-minded! God had my attention. The dream set me up for the life changing experience a few weeks later at Shalom Emporium with Messianic Rabbi Jerry Feldman. God used Jerry to break me out of **replacement theology** that had poisoned my understanding. It had been used to block my mind from receiving true revelation about the destiny of the nation of Israel in God's plan.

Paul said about his gospel, "It was by a revelation that this secret plan was made known to me. I have already written about it briefly, and if you read what I have written, you will grasp how I understand this secret plan concerning the Messiah." Ephesians 3:3-4 (CJB). So, by a dream and a revelation, I have gained an understanding of what's going on with the Jews in general, the nation of Israel in particular. With heart and faith I pray, **"Shalom Jerusalem!"**

Arrested In Shalom Emporium

It was a setup, nice day, no rain, no wind—and no warning. DeDe, my fiancée, wanted Jewish earrings to wear at the wedding. Jewish earrings—Jewish Emporium. Sounded like a match to me, so we set out for Shalom Emporium.

Mrs. Feldman helped DeDe with the earring search while I shopped about, looking at Jewish related items. The owner appeared and introduced himself as the saleslady's husband, Jerry Feldman.

What started out as a routine, **safe**, fun adventure—an earring run with "Shugah"—was about to take a stern turn. I learned something about Jews that day. They can be "sneaky-wise-dangerous." Indwelled by that resurrected Jew-Messiah, they can be downright **deadly** to your old theology. This husband-wife team waited on us with **such** servant hearts about these earrings—I never saw it coming.

Our interest moved from earrings to other items. We were being served Jesus with fresh, highly tantalizing, challenging zeal. Jerry shared the heartbeat behind the Jewish cultural life in Yeshua, his Messiah, skillfully weaving it into today's current events in the Middle East with the wisdom of God from Scripture. Each item of our interest in the Emporium was an opening for Jerry to share more. What a big heart! He wanted us to understand true meanings for today's use of these Jewish items, not just see them as external trinkets related to Jews. By now, it was obvious that his was the heartbeat of Yeshua, pumping new life to us from the Hebrew foundation of the scriptures. As my questions revealed a hunger for a better understanding of Jewish roots, Jerry opened up earnestly to share freely the wealth from his long years of study and experience. Truth burned out of him to bring God's ruling power to bear in earth in **this** generation. God had trapped me.

When Jerry's wife left for lunch, Jerry put the phone on auto-pilot and kept pouring out truth. He seated us comfortably in chairs and taught us like we were a congregation of thousands. How honored we are, I thought. Truth was hitting like a hammer into old patterns of false theology; my insides trembled and burned with fresh fire from heaven. This continued for over an hour. Yep, I was arrested—lost track o' time.

A Damascus Road experience? Close. Close to it—very close. My Baptist Seminary training did not teach me replacement theology **under that label**. ("The church **replaced** Israel in God's plan.") I didn't know it by that name; still, I had been affected by it and infected with it—and God was after it. As Jerry mentioned scripture after scripture, applying it to present-day Israel, truth shined bright enough to stun me speechless. It was **not** Jerry; it was Jesus. I had been set up, and I was being lit up. **Shame** on me!

How could I have spent four years in Seminary, majoring in Hebrew and Greek, and not have seen this? How could I have been a serious student of the Bible for half a century and missed understanding the place of Israel as a nation in God's kingdom plan? **What** an embarrassment!

For forty years, I had hammered away, preaching and writing about the kingdom of God being for now, today, in the earth—not way off in the future in some pie-in-the-sky by and by. People got mad at me for that, but God held me to it. How is it I was blinded into "spiritualizing away" the key of **earthly** Israel as a **nation** in the plan of God? I had spent more time in the prophets than any other part of the Bible. Now, almost in a flash, their burden for Israel was **so** clear. Why, all this time, had it been so very **unclear**? So **very** not clear at **all**? I thought, if I've been messed up, where's everybody else on this thing? Anyone else blinded? A few? Many? Most? None? I'm the only one? I wondered.

Scales keep falling off my spiritual eyes as I read books that Jerry suggested. Light keeps on coming; "Christian" based Babylon blackness keeps fading back out of my mind. I'm not there yet, but the murky fog has lifted from the road before me. The last big piece of the end-time puzzle has dropped into my understanding. We really **are** end-time trapped.

Jerry had preached to an international gathering of Christians and Jews in New York City what he shared with us. He didn't have a copy of that, but he said, "I did a better job covering the subject on 'For Zion's Sake' radio program last week. I have a copy of that." He found it and gave it to us. I've listened to it over and over, each time learning more. Books he suggested include Gruber's "The Church and The Jews." I found Jim Goll's "Exodus Cry" and others. I was already using Stern's "Complete Jewish Bible" and "Jewish New Testament Commentary."

Customers came in; time for us to go. My words were filled with awe and appreciation as I managed to tell Jerry, "I feel like I've been listening to a prophet of Israel. I'm honored; thank you." "Oh well," he shrugged, "I'm a Rabbi; that's what Rabbis are supposed to do, teach." Well, thank you "Officer Jerry" for teaching that day, for rising up against that flu attack and faithfully serving heaven's arrest warrant on me. I was guilty, got pardoned, but opted to "do time" anyway—making up for **lost** time. My life is now forever entwined with Israel, with the God of Abraham, Isaac, and Jacob—the Messiah of **Israel**, King of the **Jews**, God over all the earth, the David on the earthly throne in Israel, the last Adam, the Savior of all the nations.

I'm "doing time" for Israel because Israel is in God's heart. Furthermore, I take it **personally** now every time violence hurts, maims or kills in Israel. It ought **not** be so! "Who cares about little ol' Israel?" the scoffers deride. Who cares? **I do**—because **God** does—and I wrote a book to say so.

CHAPTER 2

The Jews—
Fit to be Queen

———❯◦❮———

The Lord talking to Israel in Ezekiel 16, Complete Jewish Bible: "I passed by and saw you there. I said to you, 'Live!' Yes, I said to you, 'Live! I will increase your numbers just like plants growing in the field.' And you did increase, you developed, you reached puberty, your breasts appeared, and your hair grew long; but you were naked and exposed. Again I passed by you, looked at you and saw that **your time had come, the time for love**. So I spread my cloak over you to cover your private parts and entered into a covenant with you, says ADONAI ELOHIM, and **you became mine**.

"Then I bathed you in water, washed you, and anointed you with oil.
"I also clothed you with an embroidered

gown, gave you fine leather sandals to wear,

"Put a fine linen headband on your head and covered you with silk.

"I gave you jewelry to wear, bracelets for your hands,

"A necklace for your neck, a ring for your nose,

"Earrings for your ears and a beautiful crown for your head.

"Thus you were decked out in gold and silver;

"Your clothing was of fine linen, silk and richly embroidered cloth;

"You ate the finest flour, honey and olive oil.

"You grew increasingly beautiful—you were fit to be queen.

"Your fame spread among the nations because of your beauty, because it was perfect, **due to my having bestowed my own splendor on you,**' says ADONAI ELOHIM."

What *Happened* to the Queen?

Ask one of their prophets. **Ezekiel**, what happened? **"Disgusting!"** (See Ezekiel 16 CJB)

"1, The word of ADONAI came to me: 2, Human being, **make** Yerushalayim realize **how disgusting** her practices are. 6, I passed by and saw you there, wallowing in your own blood; and as you lay in your blood **I said to you, 'Live!'** Yes, I said to you, as you lay in your blood, 'Live!'

"15, 'But you put your trust in your own beauty and began **prostituting** yourself because of your fame, **soliciting** everyone passing by and **accepting all comers**. 16, You took your clothes and used them to decorate with bright colors the high places you made for yourself, and there you **continued prostituting yourself**. Such things shouldn't happen, and in the future they won't. 17, You also took your beautiful jewels made of my gold and my silver, which I had given you, and made for yourself male images, with which you **continued to prostitute yourself**. 18, You took your embroidered clothing and covered them; you set my olive oil and my incense in front of them; 19, and you took my food, which I had given you—my fine flour, olive oil and honey, that I had given you to eat – and set it in front of them to give a pleasant aroma. That is how it was,' says ADONAI ELOHIM.

"20, 'Moreover, your sons and daughters, whom you bore me, you took and sacrificed for them to devour. Were these **fornications** of yours a casual matter? 21, **killing my children**, handing them over and setting them apart for [these idols]? 22, In all your **disgusting practices and fornications** you never remembered the condition you were in when you were young – naked, exposed and wallowing in your own blood.

"23, 'So, after this wickedness of yours – woe, woe to you!' says ADONAI ELOHIM – 24, 'You built platforms and made yourself high places in every open space. 25, You built your high places at every street corner, turning your beauty into an abomination, **spreading your legs for every passer-by,** and multiplying your acts of fornication. 26, **You had sex with your big-membered Egyptian neighbors** and engaged in fornication over and over, just to provoke me. 27, So now **I have stretched out my hand over you**, diminished your ration of food and put you at the mercy of those who hate you, the daughters of the P'lishtim, who find your **lewd behavior revolting.**

"28, ' Still unsatisfied, **you acted like a whore** also with the people of Ashur; yes, you fornicated with them and were still not satisfied. 29, You **multiplied your acts of fornication** with the land of traders, the Kasdim, and still weren't satisfied.

"30, 'You are so weak-willed!' says ADONAI ELOHIM. 'You do all these things, **behaving like a shameless whore**, 31 building your platforms on every street corner, making your high places in every open space – and yet you aren't like a whore, because you scorn getting paid. 32, Here is **a wife who commits adultery, who goes to bed with strangers** instead of her husband; 33, but also instead of receiving gifts like every other **prostitute,** you give gifts to all your lovers**, you bribe them to come to you** from all over the place and have sex with you! 34, You are the opposite of other women – **you solicit the fornication**, you aren't solicited; and **you pay them,** they don't pay you – you're the opposite!

"35, '**All right, you whore, listen to the word of ADONAI**!' 36, ADONAI ELOHIM says:

'Because your **filth** has been poured out and your **privates exposed** through your acts of **fornication** with your lovers, and because of all the idols of your **disgusting practices**, and because of the **blood of your children**, which you gave them, 37, therefore, look! I am going to gather all your lovers, to whom you have been so very nice, all the ones you hate right along with all the ones you love – I will gather them against you from all over the place and expose your private parts to them, so that they will see you completely naked. 38, I will pronounce on you the sentence that applies to women who commit adultery and murder; I will bring on you the death [decreed for] furious jealousy. 39, Yes, I will hand you over to them; and they will **make a ruin** of your platforms, **tear down** your high places, **strip you** of your clothes, **take away** your jewels, and **leave you naked and exposed**. 40, They will also **bring up a mob** against you, who will **stone you to death and hack you to pieces** with their swords. 41, They will **burn your houses to the ground** and execute judgments against you in the presence of many women. I will make you stop fornicating and you will never again pay for a lover.

"42, 'Yes, I will satisfy my fury against you. **<u>But after that</u>**, my jealousy will leave you; and I will calm down and no longer be angry. 58 You have brought it all on yourself with your **depravities and disgusting practices**,' says ADONAI.

59, "For here is what ADONAI ELOHIM says: 'I will do to you as you have done – you treated the oath with contempt by breaking the covenant. 60,

Nevertheless, **I will remember the covenant I made with you when you were a girl and will establish an everlasting covenant with you.** 61, Then you will remember your behavior and be ashamed of it **as you receive your older and younger sisters and make them your daughters**, even though the covenant with you does not cover that; 62, and **I will re-establish my covenant with you.** Then you will know that I am ADONAI; 63, so that you will remember and be so ashamed that you will never open your mouth again, so ashamed will you be **when I have forgiven you all that you have done**,' says ADONAI ELOHIM."

CHAPTER 3

Jews to Jews
Good News

———— ❧ ————

G ood news for Jews includes Ezekiel's (16:60
CJB) **"Nevertheless, I will remember the
covenant I made with you when you were a girl
and will establish an everlasting covenant with
you." Don't miss** that promise like I did years ago.
Read there again how **totally** messed up Israel was.
Could words describe it to be any worse? **In spite of
that**, God says, **"Nevertheless. . . ."** That should
encourage **us**. I need a "nevertheless" on a regular
basis.

Isaiah tells us where this "nevertheless" will
eventually lead the nation of Israel – another truth
we **must** embrace, we must **not** run over, run past,
ignore, reject, or **replace** this **Word of God!** Don't
add, don't subtract, don't **twist**. The directions read:
"Warning: Do Not Twist, Turn or Replace!"

Don't spiritualize away what **God** says through **Isaiah**, chapter 35 "¹The desert and the parched land will be glad; **the wilderness will rejoice and blossom. Like the crocus, ²it will burst into bloom;** it will rejoice greatly and shout for joy. The glory of **Lebanon** will be given to it, the splendor of **Carmel** and **Sharon**; they will see the glory of the LORD, the splendor of our God. Strengthen the feeble hands, steady the knees that give way; ⁴say to those with fearful hearts, 'Be strong, do not fear; your God will come, he will come with vengeance; with divine retribution he will come to save you.'

"⁵   Then will the eyes of the blind be opened and the ears of the deaf unstopped.

⁶   Then will the lame leap like a deer, and the mute tongue shout for joy.
    Water will gush forth in the wilderness and streams in the desert.

⁷   **The burning sand will become a pool, the thirsty ground bubbling springs.**

⁸   **And a highway will be there; it will be called the Way of Holiness.**
    No lion will be there, nor will any ferocious beast get up on it; they will not be found there. But only the redeemed will walk there, ¹⁰and the ransomed of the LORD will return.
    They will enter Zion with singing; everlasting joy will crown their heads.
    Gladness and joy will overtake them, and sorrow and sighing will flee away.'"

They will enter Zion. Israel, the Jews, the "bought back" of the Lord will enter Zion. Gentiles included? Absolutely – but **not** at the **exclusion** of the Jews, and it is the **nation** of Israel that will be restored, with Gentiles "baptized" into it through Yeshua Messiah. It is **not** the Jews "joining the church." Somebody down South made up a word— "bassackards." It meant? You guessed it—backwards (with an attitude). Satan, with his syrup factory, has had Gentiles "bassackards" about Israel's place for **centuries**. God's turning that around.

Here's a little of **Hosea's** version (chp 2) of that same vision of Israel: "⁶Therefore I will block her path with thorn bushes; I will wall her in so that she cannot find her way.

7   She will chase after her lovers but not catch them; she will look for them but not find them.

Then she will say, **'I will go back to my husband as at first,** for then I was better off than now.'

¹³ I will punish her for the days she burned incense to the Baals; she decked herself with rings and jewelry, and went after her lovers, but me she forgot," declares the LORD.

¹⁴ **"Therefore I am now going to allure her; I will lead her into the desert and speak tenderly to her.**

¹⁵ **There** I will give her back her vineyards, and will make the Valley of Achor a door of hope. **There** she will sing as in the days of her youth, as in the day she

came up out of Egypt.

16 **'In that day,' declares the LORD, 'you will call me, my husband**.' You will no longer call me, 'my master.'

18 In that day . . . bow and sword and battle I will abolish from the land, so that **all may lie down in safety.**

19 **I will betroth you to me forever; I will betroth you** in righteousness and justice, in love and compassion.

20 **I will betroth you** in faithfulness, and you will acknowledge the LORD.

23 I will plant her **for myself in the land**; I will show my love to the one I called 'Not my loved one.' I will say to those called 'Not my people, **"You are my people'**; and they will say, 'You are my God.'"

It's coming folks—let's be ready. It is written. It's coming through "from the backside o' hell," but it **is** coming.

More from Brother **Isaiah,** Chapter 54: " '[1]Sing, O barren woman, you who never bore a child; burst into song, shout for joy, you who were never in labor; because more are the children of the desolate woman than of her who has a husband,' says the LORD.

2 "Enlarge the place of your tent, stretch your tent curtains wide, do not hold back; lengthen your cords, strengthen your stakes.

3 "For you will spread out to the right and to the left; **your descendants will dispossess nations and settle in their desolate cities.**

4 "Do not be afraid; you will not suffer shame. Do not fear disgrace; you will not be humiliated.

You will forget the shame of your youth and remember no more the reproach of your widowhood.

5 **"For your Maker is your husband**—the LORD Almighty is his name—

the Holy One of Israel is your Redeemer; he is called the God of all the earth.

6 **"The LORD will call you back** as if you were a wife deserted and distressed in spirit—

a wife who married young, only to be rejected," says your God.

7 "For a brief moment I abandoned you, but **with deep compassion I will bring you back.**

8 In a surge of anger I hid my face from you for a moment, but with everlasting kindness I will have compassion on you," says the LORD your Redeemer.

9 "To me this is like the days of Noah, when I swore that the waters of Noah would never again cover the earth. So now I have sworn not to be angry with you, never to rebuke you again.

10 **"Though the mountains be shaken and the**

hills be removed, yet my unfailing love for you will not be shaken nor my covenant of peace be removed," says the LORD, who has compassion on you.

[11] "O afflicted city, lashed by storms and not comforted, I will build you with stones of turquoise, your foundations with sapphires. [12]I will make your battlements of rubies, your gates of sparkling jewels, and all your walls of precious stones.

[13] "All your sons will be taught by the LORD, and great will be your children's peace.

[14] "In righteousness you will be established: **Tyranny** will be far from you; you will have nothing to fear. **Terror** will be far removed; it will not come near you. If anyone does attack you, it will not be my doing; **whoever attacks you will surrender to you.**

[16] "See, it is I who created the blacksmith who fans the coals into flame and forges a weapon fit for its work. And it is I who have created the destroyer to work havoc;

[17] **No weapon forged against you will prevail,** (including Replacement Theology, I add.) and you will refute every tongue that accuses you. This is the heritage of the

servants of the LORD, and this is their vindication from me," declares the LORD.

And this from Jew-prophet Jeremiah, Chapter 3: 1, " 'But you have lived as a prostitute with many lovers—**would you now return to me?'** declares the LORD.

2   "Look up to the barren heights and see. Is there any place where you have not been ravished?

"By the roadside you sat waiting for lovers, sat like a nomad in the desert.

"You have defiled the land with your prostitution and wickedness.

3   "Therefore the showers have been withheld, and no spring rains have fallen.

"Yet you have the brazen look of a prostitute; you refuse to blush with shame.

6   "Have you seen what faithless Israel has done? She has gone up on every high hill and under every spreading tree and has committed adultery there. [7]I thought that after she had done all this she would return to me but she did not. [8]**I gave faithless Israel her certificate of divorce and sent her away because of all her adulteries.**

"**'Return, faithless Israel,'** declares the LORD, 'I will frown on you no longer, for **I am merciful,**' declares the LORD, 'I will not be angry forever.

13 "Only acknowledge your guilt—you have rebelled against the LORD your God, you have scattered your favors to foreign gods under every spreading tree, and have not obeyed me,'" declares the LORD.

14 **"Return, faithless people,"** declares the LORD, **"for I am your husband. I will choose you**—one from a town and two from a clan—**and bring you to Zion**. [17]At that time they will call Jerusalem The Throne of the LORD, and **all nations will gather in Jerusalem** to honor the name of the LORD. [20]But like a woman unfaithful to her husband, so you have been unfaithful to me, O house of Israel," declares the LORD.

21 "A cry is heard on the barren heights, the weeping and pleading of the people of Israel, because they have perverted their ways and have forgotten the LORD their God.

22 **"Return**, faithless people; **I will cure you** of backsliding."

"Yes, we will come to you, for you are the LORD our God.

23 **"Surely in the LORD our God is the salvation of Israel.**

Is God big enough to make his Word stick? It's not about Israel's sin and failure. It's not about **our** sin and failure. It's about God's mercy, God's faithfulness, God's audacious, bodacious love power. Be encouraged! He **is** big enough. He's big enough for Israel. He's big enough for me, and he's big enough for you. Isaiah says Israel's coming back. "Can God make it happen?" Hear what Isaiah heard before you answer.

Isaiah 40 "[1]Comfort, comfort my people, says your God.

> [2] **"Speak tenderly to Jerusalem,** and proclaim to her that her hard service has been completed, **that her sin has been paid for,** that she has received from the LORD'S hand double for all her sins.
>
> [3] "A voice of one calling: "In the desert prepare the way for the LORD; **make straight in the wilderness a highway for our God.**
>
> [4] "Every valley shall be raised up, every mountain and hill made low; the rough ground shall become level, the rugged places a plain.
>
> [5] "And the glory of the LORD will be revealed, and **all mankind together will see it. . . . .**"
>
> [6] "A voice says, "Cry out." And I said, "What shall I cry?" **"All men are like grass . . . .**
>
> [7] "The grass withers and the flowers fall, because the breath of the LORD blows on them.
> **Surely the people are grass.**

8 "The grass withers and the flowers fall, but **the word of our God stands forever**."

9 "You who bring good tidings **to Zion,** go up on a high mountain.

"You who bring good tidings **to Jerusalem,** lift up your voice with a shout,

lift it up, do not be afraid; say to the towns of **Judah**, "Here is your God!"

10 "See, the Sovereign LORD comes with power, and his arm rules for him. . .

11 "He tends his flock like a shepherd: He gathers the lambs in his arms

and **carries them close to his heart**; he **gently** leads those that have young.

12 "Who has measured the waters in the hollow of his hand, or with the breadth of his hand marked off the heavens? Who has held the dust of the earth in a basket, or weighed the mountains on the scales and the hills in a balance?

13 "Who has understood the mind of the LORD, or instructed him as his counselor?

14 "**Whom did the LORD consult** to enlighten him, and **who taught him the right way?**

"**Who was it** that taught him knowledge or showed him the path of understanding?

1 5"Surely **the nations are like a drop in a bucket; they are regarded as dust on the scales;**

he weighs the islands as though they were fine dust.

[17] **"Before him all the nations are as nothing; they are regarded by him as worthless**

and less than nothing.

[18] "To whom, then, will you compare God? What image will you compare him to?

[22] "He sits enthroned above the circle of the earth, and its people are like grasshoppers.

He stretches out the heavens like a canopy, and spreads them out like a tent to live in.

[23] **"He brings princes to naught and reduces the rulers of this world to nothing.**

[24] "No sooner are they planted, no sooner are they sown, no sooner do they take root in the ground, than he blows on them and they wither, and **a whirlwind sweeps them away like chaff.**

[25] "To whom will you compare me? Or who is my equal?" says the Holy One.

[26] "Lift your eyes and look to the heavens: Who created all these?

He who brings out the starry host one by one, and calls them each by name.

Because of his great power and mighty strength, not one of them is missing.

[27] "Why do you say, O Jacob, and complain, O Israel, "My way is hidden from the LORD; my cause is disregarded by

my God"? 28"Do you not know? Have you not heard? The LORD is the everlasting God, the Creator of the ends of the earth. He will not grow tired or weary, and his understanding no one can fathom.

29 "He gives strength to the weary and increases the power of the weak.

30 "Even youths grow tired and weary, and young men stumble and fall; 31but those who hope in the LORD will renew their strength. They will soar on wings like eagles; they will run and not grow weary, they will walk and not be faint.

Same God—same Jew—Isaiah 62 (NRSV):

1 "For **Zion's** sake I will not keep silent, and for **Jerusalem's** sake I will not rest, until her vindication shines out like the dawn, and her salvation like a burning torch. 2**The nations shall see your vindication,** and all the kings your glory; and you shall be **called by a new name** that the mouth of the LORD will give. 3You shall be a **crown of beauty** in the hand of the LORD, and **a royal diadem** in the hand of your God.

4 "You shall **no more be termed Forsaken,** and your land shall **no more be termed Desolate;**

but **you shall be called My Delight Is in Her, and your land Married;** for the LORD delights in you, and **your land shall be married.**

5 "For as a young man marries a young woman, **so shall your builder marry you,**

and as the bridegroom rejoices over the bride, so shall your God rejoice over you.

6 "Upon your walls, O Jerusalem, I have posted sentinels; all day and all night they shall never be silent. You who remind the LORD, take no rest, and **give him no rest until he establishes Jerusalem and makes it renowned throughout the earth.**

10 "Go through, go through the gates, **prepare the way for the people; build up, build up the highway,** clear it of stones, lift up an ensign over the peoples. The LORD has proclaimed to the end of the earth: **Say to daughter Zion, 'See, your salvation comes;** his reward is with him, and his recompense before him.'

12They shall be called, 'The Holy People, The Redeemed of the LORD; and **you shall be called, 'Sought Out, A City Not Forsaken.'''**

"Sought out?" Was Elijah a Jew? Could that be Elijah's Highway out, up, and away?

"Elijah's Highway"
Copyright © 2002, Daniel Gray
(Used by permission)

'68 was winding down
Martin, Dad, and Bobby all were buried like the
boys in Viet Nam
I was in the basement with the music of the spirits
Running thru me though I didn't understand
And in my new Experience I left childhood behind
My spirit opened wide as I began to lose my mind
I picked up my new instrument and started off to
find
Elijah's highway
My followers were scattered
As the devil did his dirty work and I was lying dying
in the road
Trapped there in the basement as the heebee jeebees
tortured me
To keep me from the Truth that I'd been told
A handful of adventurers said Holy Ghost was fine
The churchy people told us "don't you step across
that line"
But in our Charismania we hit the road to find
Elijah's Highway
Jimmy, Jim, and Tammy led a double-minded nation
As we learned how worldly cares can choke the
Word
Marriages were splitting just like churches as the
gifted
Ones were hearing but not doing what they heard
Reluctantly we gathered in a tiny mid-west town

We gave it everything we had though no one was around
And as the seeds were planted we were hoping we had found
Elijah's Highway
"Winter's coming early," said the Kansas City prophet
To a pastor who was looking for a change
Prophecies were flying low and someone said it thundered
And some others said, "Those people are deranged"
An Angel stood before me, and my words became more blunt
Experience is gained when you're not getting what you want
My garden tool became a sword as I marched out to find
Elijah's Highway
Ears of corn were growin and the envelope was pushing
As we fought and prayed for Babylon to fall
Some would find prosperity and others found refreshing
As revivalists were answering the call
And in the streets and prisons we would preach a better way
We threatened all the riders, we had nothing more to say
The mission rides were fine, but I was wishing I could find
Elijah's Highway
Down in Argentina there was something that was

brewing
And a blaze of fire moved across the miles
Rodney kept it growing and refreshing oil was flowing
And Canadians were laughing in the aisles
The shepherd in the cornfield couldn't make the fire start
Between the dogs attacking and the breaking of his heart
He headed down to Florida hoping he could find
Elijah's Highway
Suddenly the cornfield caught on fire and the people came
From everywhere the way that seekers would
Most of them were curious and some of them got furious
To see the church had not been as it should
And when the tiny Midwest town decided not to burn
They moved to Kansas City never to return
I followed down the road but I wishing I was on
Elijah's Highway
Churchy people criticized because they didn't realize
Believers tend to die without a dream
One by one the captains put their ships into the river
Running blindly trying to navigate that stream
So with our guns a-blazing we would ride into the night
A posse band of warriors steering ships into the light
We rode into the sunrise wishing we could realize
Elijah's Highway

Papa always told me that the churchy people need to
be
Reminded just how Babylon can be
When the Gospel Tent came down a mighty Temple
rose up
And the offering became priority
Some girls started crying saying, "Oh how can it
be?"
That's when the slayer turned around and started
slaying me
I'd finally made the grade but we were never gonna
see
Elijah's Highway
Finally they're telling me I'd lost my credibility
And winter finally melted into Spring
No more Care for anyone and everything I'd ever
done
Got swept away and didn't mean a thing
Posse put the horses up and slayer went away
Papa and the girls are silent, nothing more to say
It might be that I'm crazy or I might be on my way
To Elijah's Highway

Elijah's Highway is open. That's good news
from Jews to Jews—and all us "called crazy
Christians" who want in on it. In order for Jews to
receive the good news and hit that open Freeway,
considerable conviction and repenting ("singing the
Blues") is underway—Jeremiah leading the way.
Who's following? Besides me—and DeDe—and
Dan? Is it any wonder Jeremiah was lamenting for
Israel? "Singing the Blues" for the Jews? He **knew**
she had judgment coming her way.

My first hearing of the Blues was in the form of Negro spirituals being sung in the cotton fields of Mississippi. Toward sunset, the Negro field hands would start a low, mumbling, end-of-the-day kind of moaning. Their very **souls**, it seemed, were crying out. It always stirred me, usually deep enough for tears. They were not **legal** slaves—just an **oppressed** people in the South. Their spirits longed to soar but their culture kept clipping their wings. In their spirits they soared. I soared with 'em—**loved** their singing. It brought tears, but "joy came in the morning." Let me introduce you to the Blues in Part Two. (We're hitting on about 3 of 8 cylinders without the Blues music but we're working on the CD as God opens the way.)

Part Two: The Blues

CHAPTER 4

Let's Talk About the Blues

"Yeah-h-h-h. Jews, like us Negroes, been sangin' 'e Blues fuh a **long** time—but ain' **always** gon' be **like** dat," say Israel's prophets (Blues version). My Blues brothers, Tim and Dan, tell me of two brands o' Blues. Brand X, you keep singing over your booze 'til you bust out the bottom—"My woman done lef' me, and she hangin' out 'cross town." It's Blues that spells lose, lose, lose. But there's an upside Blues you sing on your way **up from** the losing bottom, like **coming up out** of your wilderness: "My baby lef' me all-l-l-l alone, but I got one now loves me to de bone." Anyway, we're singing Brand Upbeat. The Jews Blues is "The "Coming on **Back** Blues." **Play** yo' box, boy! **Whang** dem strangs. God got a **thang** goin' on with these Jews—getting 'em **past** singing the Blues. Take it away, Tim.

Tim: The King's Blues
Copyright © 2002 by Timothy P. Gross
(Used by permission)

1. Deep down in the fiery pits, where the devil's forced to dwell
A-plottin' and a-scheme'n to send us all to hell
He concocted a vile potion—an evil, foul notion
To use as a magic ruse, this thing he called the Blues.

2. He summoned all his minions to join him in the fray
He expressed to them opinions of how to cause decay
He doled out red hot axes to those he'd send to play
And he filled them up with lyrics of havoc and dismay

3. Without a shake or shiver this band he pointed South
To the banks of the mighty river, a sinner's city at it's mouth
Where a people long in bondage needed music they could make
And with this Devil music their souls he sought to take.

4. But at the very moment when triumph he did sense
He began to feel around him, a stillness quite intense
As he got it in his head with it's eyes so cold

and dead
To take up all his spoils of war he began to fill
with dread
5. He was blinded by a bright white light, a sear-
ing sound filled his ears
His evil mind was choked with fright, his
empty heart with fears
Cause what he saw was a band of angels come
from up on high
And with them God was rompin' on his E S
three three five
Solo
And when His licks were finished, the last note
He'd left to ring
The band dropped down in knot-tight groove
and **God** began to sing
He sang, "Listen to me Devil, my children you
can't fool
They know that I am King of all, even of the
Blues."

That's a sample of the "coming on out" kind of
Blues. Yeah, okay. It takes a little getting used to.
Stay with us.

Dan and Jeremiah Singing the Blues with the Jews

You read what happened to the Queen. They're
still "singing the Blues" under conviction. Dan
brings it into today from Jeremiah's Book of
Lamentations.

Is It Nothing To You? (Lamentations Chapter 1)
Copyright © 2002, Daniel Gray
(Used by permission)

(chorus)
Is it nothing to you, As you're passin' me by?
(repeat)
You ain't never seen anybody, Cry the way that I cry

1. The city's so lonely, How crowded it used to be
   She was a princess, Now like a widow is she
   And all her lovers and friends, Have become her enemies

2. Judah's taken captive, The roads to Zion mourn
   Her adversaries prosper, And her splendor is all gone
   They're laughing at her downfall, Those that honored now despise
   The nations are in her sanctuary, And all the people sigh

3. From above God sent a fire, And it's makin my bones burn
   My heart has been rebellious, And now it's overturned
   Nobody brings me comfort, Although they hear me sigh
   I'm feeling bad, the enemy's glad, And all I do is cry

Starving (Lamentations Chapter 4)
Copyright © 2002, Daniel Gray
(Used by permission)

1. All our gold, It was so fine but now it's not
    Our precious stones, Are like a bunch of clay pots
    And our Nazarites, Were brighter than the snow
    Unrecognizable, Now in streets we go
    (chorus)
    And the hungry ones are envious, Of those already dead
    The baby's tongue clings to it's mouth, The children have no bread
    Our skin is clinging to our bones, It's looking dry as wood
    The mothers cook their children, Cause they gotta have some food
    We are starving
2. All the kings, And the people can't believe
    That the enemy, Could make Jerusalem's people leave
    They were unclean, And then they left and went away
    "They're all gone," That's what the nations all will say
3. Our eyes have failed, And all our watching is in vain
    Watchin' for someone, Who couldn't save us from our pain
    They tracked our steps, Until we knew our

days were done
And they pursued, And now we know the end
has come

Taunting Song (Lamentations, Chapter 3)
Copyright © 2002, Daniel Gray
(Used by permission)

(Chorus)
All day long, I am their taunting song. All day long,
I am their taunting song.
(Spoken vs 1, 2 and 3)
"I am the man who has seen affliction by the rod of
his wrath.
He has led me and made me walk in darkness and
not in light.
Surely he has turned his hand against me, time and
time again throughout the day."
(Sung)
He has aged my flesh and broken my bones,
surrounded me with woe.
He has set me in a place that's totally dark, Like the
dead of long ago.
All day long, I am their taunting song. All day long,
I am their taunting song.
(Spoken, vs 16, 17, 18)
"He has broken my teeth with gravel, and covered
me with ashes.
You have moved my soul far from peace; I have
forgotten prosperity.
And I said, 'My strength and my hope have perished
from the Lord.' "

(Sung)

He has blocked my ways and hedged me in, No way to get out.

He has made my chain heavy and he shuts out my prayer, Even when I cry and shout.

All day long, I am their taunting song. All day long, I am their taunting song.

(Spoken, vs 47, 48)

"Fear and a snare have come upon us, Desolation and destruction.

My eyes flow like rivers of water, For the destruction of the daughters of my people."

(Sung)

He has turned me aside and torn me in pieces, He's bending back his bow.

He has brought me desolation and set me up, As a target for the arrow.

All day long, I am their taunting song. All day long, I am their taunting song.

(Spoken vs 58, 59, 60)

"O Lord, you have pleaded the case for my soul. You have redeemed my life. O Lord, you have seen how I am wronged. Judge my case. You have seen all their vengeance, all their schemes against me."

(Sung)

"You have heard their reproach and you know their schemes.

They whisper all day long, When you see 'em either sittin or risin up

I am their taunting song."

All day long, I am their taunting song. All day long, I am their taunting song.

But love cried out. Love keeps on crying!

Weeping Prophet (Lamentations, Chapter 5)
Copyright © 2002, Daniel Gray
(Used by permission)

(Chorus)
Well they call me the weepin prophet
Cuz I cries all day long—Cuz I cries all day long.
Listen to my Lamentations, Listen to my sad sad song.

1. They have ravished the women in Zion
   And the Judah maidens too—And the Judah maidens too
   And the musicians can't do their music—They got too much hard work to do.

2. I'm gonna write a letter, Or maybe write a book or two.
   So when you read my lamentations, Maybe you'll see what you should do.

3. Oh we pray for restoration
   From these times so hard and sad—From these times so hard and sad.
   We know God restored the last time, But this time he's really mad!
   (chorus)
   Well they call me the weepin prophet
   Cuz I cries all day long—Cuz I cries all day long.
   Listen to my Lamentations, Listen to my sad sad song.

Crying and crying and crying!

Stretched Out a Line (Lamentations Chapter 2)
Copyright © 2002, Daniel Gray
(Used by permission)

(This is the program planned **for all the earth**, this is the hand **stretched out** over all the nations. ADONAI-Tzva'ot has made his decision. **Who is there that can stop him?** He has **stretched out his hand. Who can turn it back?** See Isaiah 14:26, 27 CJB)

> (Chorus)
> Oh Mama, do you know where is the grain and wine?
> Oh Mama, do you know where is the grain and wine?
> You know the Lord's got a cloud of anger; he's done stretched out a line.

1. He has swallowed and not pitied, The place where Jacob dwells.
   He's thrown 'em down in anger, And brought 'em to the ground.
   He's standin' like an army, Bendin' back his bow.
   Swallowed up the palaces, And all the strongholds.
   (chorus)
   Oh Mama, do you know where's the grain and wine?
   Oh Mama, do you know where's the grain and

wine?

You know the Lord's got a cloud of anger; he's done stretched out a line.

2. The elders sit in silence, They throw dust on their heads.

 The children and the babies, In the streets are nearly dead.

 How shall I console you? To what can I compare?

 Your ruin's like an ocean, No one can heal you there.

 Pour out your heart like water, And don't get no relief.

 For the life of hungry children, At the head of every street.

 (chorus)

 Oh Mama, do you know where is the grain and wine?

 Oh Mama, so you know where is the grain and wine?

 You know God's got a cloud of anger; he's done stretched out a line

Part Three:
Late Gentile Dues <u>Keep</u> Jews Singing the Blues

⟫•◦•⟪

CHAPTER 5

"Gift Horse"

1.   Jacob worked for fourteen years, To bring Rachel to his side.
Laban worked for fourteen years, In a state of ambitious pride.
Jacob's work was always good, And Laban prospered there
'Til one day Jacob had enough, And couldn't be found no where.
(Chorus)
Don't abuse your gifts, Don't look a gift horse in the lips.
You'll wind up with a surprise come the dawn.
Don't abuse your gifts, Don't look a gift horse in the lips.
You might wake up one morning, And those gifts be gone.

2. Samson had the strength of God, A covenant on his head.
    Everyone who took him on, Either wound up hurt or dead.
    Delilah had the looks and charm, To really blow his mind
    And when it all was over, There was Samson weak and blind.

3. Solomon became a king, God had made him wise.
    He made him rich and handsome too, More than other kingly guys.
    He had about a thousand girls, And he tried to treat each one right.
    And when it all was over, Ol' Sol was not too bright.

4. Now every good and perfect gift, That comes from God to you
    Is something you should cherish, Not treat like number two.
    Some of those gifts are people, The Body of the Son
    But if you show them no regard, One day they might be gone.
    (Chorus)
    Don't abuse your gifts, Don't look a gift horse in the lips.
    You'll wind up with a surprise come the dawn.
    Don't abuse your gifts, Don't look a gift horse in the lips.
    You might wake up one morning, And those gifts be gone.

CHAPTER 6

Your Brother's Blood Cries

(See Genesis 4) [8] "Cain attacked his brother Abel and killed him. [9]Then the LORD said to Cain, **'Where is your brother Abel**?' 'I don't know,' he replied. **'**Am I my brother's keeper?'

[10]The LORD said, 'What have you done? Listen! **Your brother's blood cries out to me from the ground. . .'"**

From the ground comes this today also: "My dear wife. This is my good bye to you and to my treasure Lolunia and my mother. **I leave this world on the 30th/7 pm to the ovens condemned to death like a bandit.** Bronia my treasure I am sorry that I departed you believe me that I just can't write any more my hand shakes tears flooding my eyes to know I am dying like this and not guilty 58 of us are going and 10 women I kiss you for countless times and Lolunia 7 in the night remember the 30th/Oct pray say a prayer **tell Loli that daddy is gone** I can't write I can't Good bye to you and God be with you."

(Auschwitz Voices from the Ground © Copyright by Paristwowe Muzeum Oswieciw-Brezezinka and by Oficyna Wydawniza Parol Poland. These were the last words, just as he wrote them, of a husband-father burned alive in The Holocaust ovens.)

"Where is your brother Abel?" "Let's lift out the lesson here and apply it, this time to the Jew-Gentile relationship today. At this time in history, where does the Gentile church stand? **With** or **without** Israel? "Oh, I don't want to take sides," did someone say? What about God's side? Will **justice** ever cut its way through religious, bigoted theology to prevail in the **church**? Will church leaders ever quit passing prissy preacher pudding to each other and become **real** leaders? The tradition-moldy church machine **has** not, and **never will** usher in the kingdom of God. It's just **not** going to happen that way. God's got to have a **nation** into whom he can insert his passion-fired "love-gut grates," burn off a spot in earth, and police it in mercy so he can rule. Would you care to pick a nation for this—from Scripture? God needs one for a seed nation.

Anyone pick one? Got a problem with God working in unredeemed Jews, unredeemed Israel? How about unredeemed Americans? Unredeemed America? Consistency requires that we apply the same to America. Who argues for America being a redeemed nation? Yet, we sure pray God works in America, right? Just so, God can work in Israel to bring her into her **God-promised, scripture-written destiny.** What about the **redeemed** in Israel? God already has a little redeemed Gideon-gathering of **Messianic** Jews, leavening the national lump. They live every breath under the gun—understaffed, under-financed, under-supported in prayer, under everything, but still, under **God** they will possess the nation for him. Why all the "unders" for these key players in God's plan? Where's their Gentile side of the family, the "church?"

Where **are** we? We're **busy**—in the **opposite** direction—away from Israel—expecting Israel to "join the church."

> God: "Where is your brother Abel?"
>
> "Churchianity": "Am I my Jewish brother's keeper? We have **Jesus** now."

Oh! "Churchianity's" not **saying** that? If they're **not**, they're **doing** that, and **many** of them are **saying** that in their stand on Israel. No open stand **for** is an obvious stand against. Remember the church's silence during The Holocaust? Recently, someone told me how a big denominational church by the railroad track saw Jews, their arms waving out of cattle cars, screaming and begging, "Help us! Somebody, please help us!" They were being hauled to concentration camps in Germany—to The Holocaust. The church became very upset by the crying and pleading of regular daily trainloads going by and responded. Their response? **They planned** their services so the begging wouldn't disturb their worship service; they sang hymns louder to drown out their cries! "The LORD said, "What have you done? Listen! **Your brother's blood cries out to me from the ground.**"

However you slice it and dice it, the following scripture is tough: (See Matthew 7)

[21]"Not everyone who says to me, 'Lord, Lord,' will enter the kingdom of heaven (on earth). . . . [22]**Many** will say to me on that day, 'Lord, Lord, did we not **prophesy** in your name, and in your name **drive out demons** and **perform many miracles**? (Why, **that** could be Charismatic Christians.) [23]Then I will tell them plainly, '**I never knew you. Away from me, you evildoers!**'

[24]"Therefore everyone who hears these words of mine and **puts them into practice** is like a wise man who built his house on the rock. [25]The rain came down, the streams rose, and the winds blew and beat against that house; yet it did not fall, because it had its foundation on the rock. [26]But everyone who hears these words of mine and **does not put them into practice** is like a foolish man who built his house on sand. [27]The rain came down, the streams rose, and the winds blew and beat against that house, and **it fell with a great crash.**"

"**I never knew you. Away from me, you evildoers!**" What do you do with this line, and this whole passage? Yes, "knew" means intimate or experiential knowledge. "Evildoers" carries the weight of "doing your own thing, not God's." It includes those who do **not** put into practice the words of Jesus, operating instead on their own plan. God's plan brings Israel back to God for God to use them in nation-reaping, (unless you cut out the Old Testament, the prophets, Apostle Paul, and some other Jews).

Well, rains **will** come, streams **will** rise, winds **will** blow and batter. I don't want my house to fall with a great crash. I don't want to hear Jesus say, "Who **are** you? You didn't work with me on my kingdom plan to get my Jewish family back. You've got your **own** 'ministry,' **remember?** Get on **away from me** and take your ministry with you!" **Anybody** want to hear that? I will **not** hear that, and my house will **not** fall with a great crash. Where's my brother Abel? He lives again in Israel, in the David Lazarus pastors, and in the remnant of Jews. Israel is where his blood first cried out; that's where his blood **still** cries out. That's why **I** cry out, **"Yes Lord!** I **am** my brother Abel's keeper! Shalom Jerusalem.

CHAPTER 7

Longstanding Land Deal

❯◦❮

God made dirt. Then he made humankind out of dirt. He called the making place **Eden**. His humans gave themselves to the devil, and the devil got the dirt in the deal. God still liked his dirt so he kept talking to folk about it. **Finally,** somebody listened; his name was Abraham. God said, "Abraham, somebody else is living on my dirt. I want it back. Will you be my friend and help me get it back? I'll cut a deal with you. I'll supply the God-power; you supply the manpower. I'll take it back through you and share the Garden of Eden with you and your downline forever. How 'bout it?" Abraham said, **"Deal!"**

That deal **will** go down; it will close. Man may invent disrupting doctrines of "spiritual Israel," "raptures," "comings" and such; he may go on about who's going where and when—who's doing what when. **No matter**; none of it will keep God from pulling off this land deal. If time runs out before the deal comes about, God will just make some **more** time—no biggy—he wound the first clock. He's **eternal**. He's Alpha and Omega; He can work both ends **and** the middle until it all comes back around like he likes it.

I'm thinking, "What's the purpose of this physical creation?" Is it not for God to reveal Himself, not just **to**, but **into** a "substance" setting? Is it not for God to have a place and a people he can live in physically and perpetuate forever—and finally end up with his creation on display throughout the ages for his glory? If not, then what? What's it for? If God's purpose **is** to have a garden setting in which to enjoy his creation, do you figure he'll get tired and give up the idea? I mean, think a minute. If you were God and you wanted something, what-'n-who could keep you from having it? That's why I'm **not** expecting this physical creation to disappear in a cloud of **anything**—not before God gets what God started out to get—a garden full of his "image and likeness" beings.

Oh, Dr. Watts, where are you? (J. Wash Watts, Professor of Old Testament and Hebrew, New Orleans Baptist Theological Seminary, a Hebrew scholar highly regarded, even by Orthodox Jewish scholars.) **Why** didn't I keep my notes from your Hebrew class 45 years ago? Dr. Watts taught from the Hebrew text like Jesus taught, with **authority:** "God promised the **land** to Abraham and his descendants

forever. That's embedded in the root meaning of the Hebrew words themselves. It's in the **language** itself, **not** just the content of the promise. He gave the **land, the dirt,** to Abraham and his descendants forever. Make no mistake about it; **God promised** the land itself to Israel." Why didn't I **listen** to the "Baptist Israelite?"

What **was** it that Apostle John looked at and had to write about? Ah-h-h, a **new** heaven and a **new** earth. We're not talking about **how** this comes about; we **are** taking notice that God gets **land** again— "new **earth, dirt**" (although some seem to suppose "new earth" to be dirtless. Dirtless **earth**?) John heard a great voice out of heaven saying, in effect, "Look John, God's back on earth again, living among men. He's got his garden back; it's filled with his very own people. Abba's family is all gathered around him." Oh yeah, he's got it coming, a garden just to his liking. From this in Revelation 21 (as well as Isaiah and others), I can see a new "garden-earth" headed this way.

Think about it: new garden, new earth, new heaven, new Jerusalem through a **new** Adam, Jesus Christ—through a new humanity, new civilization. I'm persuaded **this** generation includes enough lovers to kick killer-Adam and kiss the last One. Hello Eden; hello Jerusalem. Hello Alpha-Eden; hello Omega-Jerusalem! God's cutting 'cross-country to keep his longstanding land deal with his friend, Abraham and kin—and all their friends.

CHAPTER 8

Paul, Why Gentiles?

———————

Saul of Tarsus, Christian stalker-killer, converted
to Paul, apostle to the Gentiles. Why? Why,
Paul? Why Gentiles? Let's start with:

> Jews—Gentiles
>
> **The** Jew—Jew**s**

The Jew (Gentiles call him Jesus) was born a
Jew, grew up a Jew. Could the following have
happened? His mother tasted the water and went,
"Hmm. **Yeshua**! Have you been praying over the
drinking water again? We **do** need one pot of **plain**
water, you know" (from a Dan Gray sermon). He
was a Jew—far as I know, still is. Jews are his
kinfolk. Jesus likes Jews.

Paul was a Jew. He said of himself, "(I am) of
the people of Israel, of the tribe of Benjamin, **a
Hebrew of Hebrews**; in regard to the law, a
Pharisee. . . (Phil 3:5) Paul was Jew to the bone.
Speaking generally, there are two groups of people

in the world: Jews and Gentiles. Where you fit is fairly easy. If you don't **know** you're a Jew, chances are, you're a Gentile, a **non**-Jew.

Paul is an Abraham (of sorts) to the Gentiles, first "sent-one" to come after us. In that sense, he "fathered" us in Yeshua, **The** Jew. Are you with me now? Okay. Question: Which direction does Paul take us Gentiles? Do you find Paul repeatedly telling Gentiles that he's our apostle to bring us to Jesus **so we can have a sweet, sweet home in heaven someday?** Is he hawking, "Step right up, ladies and gentlemen. Get your free ticket to heaven 'cause you could die tonight?" Or, did he point us back to Abraham as **our** father of faith, same as Jews?

He **does** say this (See Romans 9):

"[2]I have great sorrow and unceasing anguish in my heart. (After years in the desert with God, he came out burning with this.) [3]For I could wish that I myself were **cursed and cut off from Christ** for the sake of my brothers, those of my own race, [4]**the people of Israel.**"

(See all of Romans 11):

"[1]I ask then: **Did God reject his people?** By no means! I am an Israelite myself, a descendant of Abraham, from the tribe of Benjamin. [2]**God did not reject his people,** whom he foreknew.

"[5]So too, **at the present time there is a remnant** chosen by grace.

"[11]Again I ask: **Did they stumble so as to fall beyond recovery? Not at all!** (Well Paul, why are you going to the **Gentiles** then?). . . salvation has come to the Gentiles **to make Israel envious.** (Why did God send Paul to the Gentiles? "to make Israel envious.")

"¹³I am talking to you Gentiles. Inasmuch as I am the apostle to the Gentiles, I make much of my ministry ¹⁴**in the hope that I may somehow arouse my own people to envy and save some of them**. (Why? "in the hope of saving Jews.")

"¹⁷You (Gentiles), though a wild olive shoot, have been grafted in among the others and now share in the nourishing sap from the olive root. **You do not support the root, but the root supports you.** (The root, Israel, supports the non-Jew church.)

"²⁵I do not want you to be ignorant of this mystery, brothers (Gentiles). . .

"²⁶**all Israel will be saved**, as it is written: **God's gifts and his call are irrevocable.** They too have now become disobedient in order that they too may now receive mercy **as a result of God's mercy to you.**" (How will Israel be saved? Through Gentiles who have received God's mercy.)

God did **not** send Paul to us Gentiles primarily to get us to heaven when we die. He did it "to make Israel envious," in the hope of somehow arousing Israel to envy to save a Jewish remnant to possess all Israel—to save all Israel. God **promised** to restore Israel. "God's gifts and his call are irrevocable." God planned and **hopes** to use us to do **something** in his love and mercy to save Israel.

CHAPTER 9

What I Do About <u>The</u> Jew—What I Do About the Jews

———➤❖◄———

Matthew 7:21ff (THE MESSAGE)

"Knowing the correct password—saying 'Master, Master,' for instance—isn't going to get you anywhere with me. **What is required is serious obedience—*doing* what my Father wills.** I can see it now—at the Final Judgment thousands strutting up to me and saying, 'Master, we preached the Message, we bashed the demons, our God-sponsored projects had everyone talking.' And do you know what I am going to say? **'You missed the boat. All you did was use me to make yourselves important. You don't impress me one bit. You're out of here.'"**

What does this scripture mean? I don't **want**

Jesus to say that to me! "What is required is serious obedience—**doing** what my Father wills." I long to **do** that—about **everything**. I long to **do** in my life what Father wills about Israel and the Jews in my time—serious obedience for serious kingdom business. I reached the conclusion that these are my most critical decisions:

1. What I do about the Jew
2. What I do about the Jews

The Jew is Messiah Yeshua; the Jews are his first-family, his chosen nation. Jesus came as Messiah of **Israel,** King of the **Jews**. God let the rest of us in on the same Jew deal, **not** for us to call for a new Gentile deal and a new deck. **We** cooked up the Christianity hodgepodge, separate from Jewish roots. Let's get real. Hodgepodge hasn't worked for a near-2000, and it's **not** working now. More of what's **not** working is **not** the solution. **That—is— not**—the solution! It's **high** time we got outside Stuporville City Limits and checked the map.

There we can find Jesus talking to Nicodemus (John 3), "Nic, you and all Israel have to go back— back, back—back beyond outward carcasses, scraps and all, back beyond religious ritual, traps and all— back to the **heart** of worship, back into the beginning, into Father's **heart,** and come out 'born fresh from the beginning.' It has to happen that way." I find Gentiles with some "going back" to get done— along with Nic and his nation.

The whole Bible needs to be re-chewed and "re-Jewed." David H. Stern helped me—his Complete Jewish Bible and New Testament Commentary—

wonderful, scholarly "re-Jewing" of the Word. **Thank you, brother David!** His love-labor is only the beginning of the "re-Jewing" needed to **upset** the church in order to **set up** the church in God's plan. Why upset the church? Because it slipped off its foundation—and never knew it. Because ignorant, biased, anti-Semitic **stuff** is the poison in the pot. Demons have force-fed us this filth for centuries, and bloated the whole Gentile world, **church included**, into gloating arrogance. Which of our Christian "giants" has stood up and answered this question right? "What do I do about the Jews?" I **know** this: we **dare not** risk a final face to face appearance with the God of Abraham, Isaac, Jacob, David, and Yeshua without having **their** God's heart about Israel and the Jews. It flat-out won't do; we best "re-(J)chew." "What is required is serious obedience—*doing* what my Father wills." "The King will reply, 'I tell you the truth, whatever you did for one of the least of these brothers of mine, you did for me.'" (Matthew 25:40)

Did I hear, "That doesn't apply to Jews in general?" Then how about Jews in particular? Namely, those laboring **with** Messiah Yeshua against humanly insurmountable odds—in Israel and elsewhere? Those **marked** as the remnant for Jesus to use to reclaim Israel for Father? Death droops over their doorsteps, death dogs their foot-steps to the store, hounds them to school, to work, to their Messianic Congregations. What is Gentile Christendom doing for these Jews? When we do for the Jews, we do for **The** Jew. Then, when it's all said and done, we find we did something for ourselves, our family, our church, our nation, our **generation, our God!**

I really don't know why God mercifully tapped me to type out this. I was guilty as a dog! I confess: blinded by seminary-slickened theology, I paid Israel a passing prayer; that was about it. Didn't exactly **say** the church replaced Israel, just **lived** like it did. Then, **one** day—whoa! God **did** show—got my goat **good!** Now, I'm trusting serious obedience to keep me on course to do what Father revealed, and enable me to help someone else presently snagged in my old briar patch. I mean, I just plain did not **know**—yep, ignorant. God revealed, and I peeled—layer after layer—of old mindsets. I missed the boat first time around, but God-of-the-second-chance called again. I'm on the boat now with the Jew and the Jew-crew. I heard Cap'n, "All a-boa-oa-oard! **La-a-a-ast call!**"

CHAPTER 10

The Mighty GTC (Gentile Titanic Church)

———➤•◄———

I stood propped up on two crutches. He stood in front of me, the most passionate living Jew I ever encountered. "Surely," I thought, "Somehow Elijah's back—in front of me—or is this Paul? Or fiery Peter? Or John?" My insides trembled under the impact as scripture after scripture hit bulls-eye-center in my innermost-bottom. Rabbi Jerry Feldman's intensity never lessened for ninety minutes. He wasn't just delivering a message; he **was** a message, **on fire**. What was the message? **Messianic** Jews are crying and dying. The church's interest as a body makes **not a ripple, not a sound.** I remembered Hitler's "whole burnt offering" (Holocaust) of millions of Jews. What did the church do then? They stood right where the trains unloaded the victims (I saw a photograph.) and sang Christian hymns to celebrate what **they** said was **God** cleansing the earth of "Jesus-killing" Jews. Can you **imagine!** They **watched** and celebrated men, women, and children walking, and babies being carried:

- ♦ To gallows to be hanged, or
- ♦ To other gallows where their hands were tied behind them, bodies flipped to hang upside down till they choked to death, or
- ♦ To "showers" where gas pellets were dropped in on them to form a gas that ruptured their insides, causing them to hemorrhage to death after more than an hour of agonizing pain, or
- ♦ To an enclosed area to face a firing squad, or
- ♦ To "experimental rooms" to be "experimented" to death in all kinds of bizarre brutality, or
- ♦ To huge, open graves, sixty feet deep, to be buried, some alive, by the hundreds, or
- ♦ **To ovens to be cooked alive!**

How **many?** Give or take a few thousand human lives—Jews and non Jews—**twenty million (20,000,000)** in just six years—1939-1945. "Well, it **couldn't** have been **that** bad." Who **said** that, anyhow? Tell them to **go get some history, and get real!** Go to The Holocaust Museum and **learn** something—or, you know what? We're destined for a **way-worse** repeat. The demon's still dancing and wallowing in rage—I saw him in that dream—and heard him scream, "**Cook me some more Jews.**"

He's not just in dreams—and he didn't just live in Hitler and Stalin. He's living in, raging in, human bodies whose hearts are fired with religious fervor, whose minds are twisted and molded into snake-Satan shape, whose lives are demon driven to die for their dastardly, "fatherless" beliefs. **We best wake up!** The **very** same Haman and all his buddies are busy as bees in the Middle East **even as you read this.** Now the names are the likes of the Ben Ladins, Arafats and Saddams, rather than the Hitlers and Stalins, but the **mindset** is **absolutely** the same—and worse than **that?** The mindset of **"the church"** is **exactly** what it was when Hitler and Stalin were butchering **sixty a second for six years**—9,000 a day—270,000 a month—3,333,333 a year—for six years—20,000,000 in all—and who gave a rap 'round the world? Who got involved to stop it? Who's getting involved today—to the point of changing one single thing in their daily lives or their churches? Think about it. Those who don't learn from history—are what? You know the quote. Destined for a repeat. It's coming—catch the news tonight at your house. Will any changes take place in you as you watch? In your heart? In your home? In your church? In your ministry? **Last** millennium would have been better for us to wake up—but it's gone.

So the church sang while Jews burned. Again, what about today? Today, **what? What and who!** Have **you** seen, heard, or read of any church outcry against the violence against Jews in 2002? **God,** in his shalom mercy, turned around this headed-the-wrong-way Gentile a few months ago.

This "Damascus Road" experience left me forever changed. It did for me what **sixty** years of Bible study didn't do, what **fifty** years in church ministry didn't do, what **five** years in Baptist Seminary did **not** do, what Greek and Hebrew studies did **not** do. It **convicted** me into a 180 degree correction-turn of my Christian belief about today's Israel. It **continues** to build in me the absolute certainty that **the entire organized, institutional church rides the "The Mighty Gentile Titanic Church."** Simply put, we're cruising on "sunk-already!" Just a matter of minutes, heaven's time. That's why I'm being—what? "Forceful?" Is that a good word—about this? "Nice" didn't really reach me all that time, and, looking around, I don't see the smooth and suave sisters having much affect in the church's direction. I'm **compelled** to do something—and this is it. This church ship's overrun with celebrities, totally blinded by program-partying. Destruction's jaws are jacked wide. We've **got** to get off the bastard-boat, sink it and free-float—in God's hand and plan. Better to feel helpless in God-obedience now than be helpless in God-wrath down the road.

Look for the lifeboats—hanging there to save "Noah's eight" survivors. Is it too late to turn? Yes it is! Too late to turn "The Mighty GTC," for **who can turn her?** To **whom** will she listen? **Not** to the old prophets: "Old Testament prophecy types have no place in the church age," they tell you. **Not** to present-day prophets: "The prophetic? It's pathetic," they joke. Then they mock, they laugh—and build bigger buildings, bigger programs, bigger "ministry" empires. Every church does what's right in its own eyes, and The GTC speeds heedlessly ahead, loaded with unsuspecting "believers" in her sanctity. It's gone, I tell you—done, sunk. You think **you** can turn her, do you? Go ahead; waste your life talking about how Christ loves this GTC monster that **Satan** calls the church. It is **not** the true church. Christ will marry **that? It "ain't gonna" happen!** I'd concentrate on the life boats, my friend. They'll hold a remnant.

What was my 180 about? God's **indestructible** Word on **those indestructible Jews!** The GTC crew should **never** have taught me God was finished with the **nation** of Israel. **Never** should have said, "Forget Israel, the nation; we have Jesus." Did I wheel around 180 because of my own great love for Jews? No, absolutely not. Because Jerry was my best friend, and a persuasive orator? **No!** I turned because I **got** turned, by **God Himself.** The Jew, Prophet Jerry, spoke for **The** Jewish Prophet, and for all the true prophets of old. **Truth** fell like hot coals into my boiler room and **burned** my ship around, just in the nick o' time. I'm writing this to load the lifeboats. It's time to **jump ship, folks**. The proud die loud—**screaming**-loud. The humble bow way on down, grab who they can, and get off a drunken-skippered ship full of Jew-refusing rebels. Turn 'em, Lord, turn 'em—like you turned me!

GTC directions are set in religious concrete, **without** Israel. You can turn some **people**, but you'll **never** turn that GTC **machine**. Who **needs** it! Not God—and he's not about to save it. "**Our**

Own-thing" flags fly high, ship-wide on the GTC. "Jews? Who needs 'em,?" the crew asks. "We'd let 'em board if we could make room without **upsetting** anybody," her skipper says. **That's backwards!** God's plan requires Gentiles to board Israel's ship ("wild" Gentiles grafted into the original, cultivated tree. God's been cultivating Israel for a **long** time.) We've been backwards ever since our "great church fathers" got together a thousand years ago with their nose in the air about Jews. Church gatherings, featuring festering attitudes still follow suit, centuries later, pouring in more of their church-replaced-Israel concrete into the GTC. It'll sink her. Don't go down with her.

Quit taking up for that impending disaster and **get off it!** To make this sinkable GTC "stayable" is outright stinkable, downright unthinkable. Haul down a lifeboat for your friends. If you have to, **dive overboard by yourself**, and swim like heaven toward a ship with an Israel-hearted Captain. Save your soul; The Mighty GTC's down in God's stormy waters.

CHAPTER 11

Destination: Away!

The "Gentile Titanic Church" (GTC) is the star-ship in the Babylon fleet. She boasts the finest men's minds can muster—brags of plying the waters with flying flags forever. Who can compare? Dispute her sea worthiness, who would dare? She's the Queen ship; her decks and suites brimming with proud celebrants of her indestructibility. Ah, but what's that up ahead? **She's** clueless, and reckless—overconfidently giddy to stupidity, because the indestructible is about to –

But first, what **about** this GTC?" Her makers were the movers and shakers among the "church fathers," intellectuals weary of Jews "bringing shame" on their Gentile churches. They mind-made this non-Jew people-holder and launched her with great fanfare and scholarly wisdom of man's theology. Great minds of the church had spoken; people lined up to board. They trusted "great minds."

A few dared ask, "Why are we leaving out the Jews? Why include all nations except God's seed nation? What about **God's** plan for the **salvation** of the Jews?" Our "great" church fathers spouted their new-found theological answers—scholarly sounding, intellectually challenging, but confusing. Those who refused the confused, leave-out-the-Jew plan were barred from boarding, branded as rebellious heretics, and mercilessly "cursed" and killed. "The ship must sail," spoke the mighty Gentile leaders. "Gentile Titanic" launched from the dock of pride, prejudice, hatred, division, and murder. Destination? "Kingdom of Heaven," they **said**. "**This** ship?" God snorted!

Aboard "The Mighty GTC," some of us tried to wade through centuries of rapture teachings, second coming theories, and mountains of intellectual millennial disputing, hoping somehow to find **meaning** and destiny somewhere in it. In such theological underbrush, we got no vision of God on lookout for somebody on earth to take the thing **back** for him. The GTC crew was schooled to steer clear of those waters. They charted a **get-away** course, their theological maps pointing **away** from earth toward heaven, **away** from the present-day to the "someday," and above all, **away from those detestable, despicable Jews!**

So the GTC's been afloat for a-while now. God's been ever so merciful for her to get rid of national and cultural prejudice—but she hasn't. Her crew just looked the other way with a "you can't fight the captain" shrug. The GTC seethed unrest, but the ship sailed on, **never** changing course. Jew-loving "trouble makers" were dealt with, and the ship sailed on—always **away** from the Jews, **away** from loving Israel as a key player in God's end-time game plan.

There were times when men managed to smuggle God aboard the GTC. Cleansing began; signs, wonders, miracles happened. The GTC captain and crew deftly doused the fire, never changing directions, and the ship sailed on. She stubbornly held her no-nation-of-Jews course. God got off, but nobody noticed, 'cause the ship sailed on. Poor God! What do you **do** with such a ship and crew? I have different questions. Why do we think God has to have this Babylon-based delusion of confusion? Who told us God **has** to save her? Who **needs** it anyhow?

Wait up a minute now, 'fore you get all riled up. Let's ask, "Who wants a ship full of **God's** presence? His love? His peace? Joy? With miracles? Healings? Signs and wonders?" Let's go figure. What's God likely to do about GTC if he's **not** welcome to do what **he** wants, **with** whom he wants, **how** he wants? Oh sure, he'll come personally to individuals who cry out, but what of the **ship**? With God **not** welcome on the ship?

What if God has launched **his** ship, flying the Star of David, his Jew God-Son wearing the Captain's cap? What **then**? Hello glory! This is the ship for me. God's engulfed the whole vessel with **his** presence, doing **his** thing. **His** heart is yearn-burning to give **his** very self to all his shipmates. This is the one for me. It's harbored in Israel, catching **High** Wind, sailing **High** seas, centered in God's creative plan for the nations and the world. Come on, God of Abraham, Isaac, Jacob, David, and Father of David-Yeshua; **we got you trusted!**

CHAPTER 12

Storm Dead Ahead

———————➤•➤•◄•———————

Young, red-headed Shelley stood broken, weeping, trembling as she preached to hundreds in the regular Sunday night IHOP service in Kansas City. It was not the fear of man that made her tremble. "Jesus showed up in my room," she said, "with a burning torch in each hand."

None of us can shake off the ship-in-the-storm warning that followed from Jesus. The storm was a ferocious super-storm—boiling black clouds, flashing and shooting fire beyond human imagination, raging wildly, from water level up to fill all the skies. The ship was full speed ahead right into it. "Jesus thrust the two torches, fear and first-love, deep down in me," she said. Then he commanded with bone-burning authority, "You go tell IHOP and the nation what **I'm** saying, and what **you're** seeing." Shelley saw herself, floundering alone in the water, helplessly staring directly into the oncoming ship, the storm behind her. How could she turn so great a ship from so fierce a storm?

Then this past Sunday morning at Christ Triumphant Church, Hal was preaching; "Turn to Romans 9:1," he said; I did, in my Complete Jewish Bible: ". . . my grief is so great, the pain in my heart so constant, that I could wish myself actually under God's curse and separated from the Messiah, **if it would help** my brothers, my own flesh and blood, **the people of Israel!"**

Hal's going on. I'm stuck on the next verse, "They were made **God's children**, the **Sh'khinah** has been with them, the **covenants** are theirs, likewise the giving of the **Torah** (law), the **Temple** service and the promises; the **Patriarchs** are theirs; and **from them. . .** came the **Messiah**. . . .

I remembered Paul's argument in 11:1, "Isn't it that God has repudiated his people?" Answer, "Heaven forbid! **God has not repudiated his people.** Quite the contrary, it is by means of their stumbling that the deliverance has come to the Gentiles, **in order to provoke them to jealousy.** (so **that's** how Gentiles got included!) Moreover, if Israel's being placed **temporarily** in a condition less favored than that of the Gentiles is bringing riches to the latter—how much greater riches will **Israel in its fullness** bring them!"

Has anybody **ever** topped Paul's commitment to go get Gentiles for God? Any with more scars, more fruit? What fueled such passionate intensity for the Gentiles? Great grief, constant heart pain for **Jews.** (vs.1) Paul goes on, "in the hope that somehow I may **provoke** some of my own people **to jealousy** and save some of them." (vs. 14) Pick up verse 25, "For, brothers (Gentile brothers this time), I want you to understand this truth which God formerly concealed but has now revealed**, so that you (Gentile Christians) won't imagine you know more than you actually do**. It is that stoniness, **to a degree**, has come upon Israel, **until** the Gentile world enters in its fullness; and that **it is in this way** that **all Israel will be saved**."

Shelley saw the ship as American Christianity, including IHOP. So what is the fire-filled storm, looming dead ahead? Since I had already written most of the above chapters on the "Gentile Titanic Church" while working on writing-class assignments, I took the encounter to heart. The timing was too exact to be coincidental. (God has urged us along throughout this writing with weekly, sometimes nightly, confirmations from others.) I didn't have to interpret the meaning for **me**. It came applying itself into me! Paul **never** said God's plan was church **instead of** the nation of Israel. "Until the Gentile world enters in its fullness" (above) could well mean "Until God pulls in enough Gentiles to 'midwife' Israel into her destiny." He could have enough now **to** do it, if they **would** do it. Paul saw God gathering Gentiles into congregations **in order to** reach back **through** Gentile congregations to "provoke Israel to jealousy." Through Gentile congregations, God brings his wife back into his heart. Then, from Israel, his heart, he pours out his love (and cleansing judgment) over creation and rules it.

Is America's church-ship pointed in **that** direction, or is it pointed full-speed **away** from Israel, with a doggedly determined mindset to possess the kingdom for itself, **separately** from the Jews, **and** on its own going-away-from-Jews Gentile turf? You know the answer when you stop and think, but there's a busy church ear-plugger that would love to run you on past stopping and thinking. Don't let it. The Gentile church is **not** losing sleep 'cause her mama's losing blood in the street. Shouldn't Gentile congregations be backing Messianic congregations, like Pastor David Lazarus's in Israel, like Jerry Feldman's here, helping them birth God's chosen **nation** for the **Jews** to bring in the end-time harvest of souls like God's plan calls for?

What is the Gentile church's **God-given** mandate for Israel? Is it just to include Israel, **along with, and on equal standing,** with all other nations? Is it just to do an "Israel Mandate" whenever we can fit it in with everything else, **or should the "Israel Mandate" be the heart and centerpiece?** Shelley's storm says to all shipmasters, **"Swing 'er around, Captain, or you're going down!** You'll end up on the bottom of the sea of people with the rest of the ships sailing out of Babylon. **Focus** full Gentile church strength around, and **center** it on getting Israel back into God's heart. A storm of the magnitude sent to Shelley is God's warning of his long overdue, roaring wrath against the mutinous Gentile ship, overrun with mutineers for 1900 years, running away, with the Captain chained in the ship's bowels. **Abba, Himself,** is storming on-scene with a heaven full of shofar-blowing angels, blasting out: "You imagined you knew more than you actually did until you **wore me out**. Now free this Captain and **turn this ship around!**"

CHAPTER 13

You Missed the Boat

Three Scriptures:

1. (Again): Matthew 7:21ff (THE MESSAGE) "Knowing the correct password—saying 'Master, Master,' for instance—isn't going to get you anywhere with me. What is required is serious obedience—*doing* what my Father wills. I can see it now—at the Final Judgment thousands strutting up to me and saying, 'Master, we preached the Message, we bashed the demons, our God-sponsored projects had everyone talking.' And do you know what I am going to say? **'You missed the boat. All you did was use me to make yourselves important.** You don't impress me one bit. **You're out of here.'"**

2. 1 Cor 12:13: "For we were all baptized **by (in, or with) one Spirit into one body**—whether Jews or Greeks, slave or free—and we were

all given the one Spirit to drink."

3. 1 Cor 12:13. (THE MESSAGE) "By means of his one Spirit, we all said goodbye to our partial and piecemeal lives. We each used to independently call our own shots, but then we entered into a large and integrated life in which he has the final say in everything. . . . Each of us is now a part of his resurrection body, refreshed and sustained at one fountain—his Spirit—where we all come to drink. **The old labels we once used** to identify ourselves—labels like Jew or Greek, slave or free—are **no longer useful. We need something larger, more comprehensive."**

"You missed the boat. All you did was use me to make yourselves important. You don't impress me one bit. You're out of here." Not words I want to hear Jesus say to me, not now, not **any time**. I don't want to miss the boat; neither do I want to get caught on the wrong one. The old labels we once used to identify ourselves—labels like (Charismatic, Christian, Catholic, Baptist, Fundamental, Evangelical)—are no longer useful. We **must have** "something larger, more comprehensive"—like "One body flowing together and drinking together in his One Holy Spirit."

You know that humongus, centuries-old, grindingly cumbersome monstrosity of a church **machine**? The one committee-ed-to-death, and committed forever to propagating committees—to study everything and everybody to death and **do** nothing? **That** one. I just **know** it's the **wrong** one. I am **not** missing God's **Spirit**-boat again. Call me rebellious, non-submissive, independent, church-hopper—you'll **not** get me off God's one-**Spirit**, one-body boat.

Look at how many preachers are deceived, thrashing, and bouncing about in traditional trash. So very sad, and **bad** it **is**, that many are **using** God to make themselves important by building a great "ministry," a great megachurch empire, or **what** ever! **Sickening**, I say. Why do we keep putting up with it? Well, I'm **not**. God lifted my head out of the ostrich sand, I rubbed the grit out, and **got** out, like **God** did. Took me longer, but I finally did. It's best for all concerned that we **not** help the blinded (or mule-headed) build bigger batches to boost the Babylon boat.

Oh, and this **really** scares me: many of these ambitious, leader, ladder-climbers are **using God and** Jews in the present scenario to make **themselves** important: "Oh, we just **love** the Jews." ("Master, Master": password stuff) Watch to see if they're **doing** what Father wills, or if it's all just a most clever, cooked up, heart wrenching gimmick to use God and the Jews to build bigger **"my"** church, **"my"** ministry, **"my"** worldwide spiritual base— "my, my, me, me." Oh my, oh me! **Whoa, whoa— woe!** Hello **Jehu**! Where are **you**, good-buddy Jew? **Come ride today!**

Anyone can come out of that church-crunch-bunch. Look for **Spirit and Life-truth**. It may be a **no** name "move." It **could** be "THE CALL," "IHOP," or "ONE THING," or **some other** whoever-heard-of-**that**-before handle. It's not the handle; it's the **moving**, it's the **flowing** that'll keep you going—with **God**, not with the let's-get-this-over-with-for-another-week church throng, listening for the dinner gong.

For those rallying to religious program-partying, squirming their heads deeper into the sand of sick machinery "to save the church": be warned. These words are still out there burning: "You missed the boat. All you did was use me to make yourselves important (or comfortable). You're out of here." I **don't-want-to-hear-em; I got gutted up, got out!** Paid dearly, I did—**but I'm off the ostrich farm.** (FYI: Word has it that Babylon Conglomerate "bought the farm.")

CHAPTER 14

His Feet <u>Will</u> Stand There

⟹►◦◄⟸

(See Zechariah 14:4, 9) "**⁴On that day his (Adonai's) feet will stand on the Mount of Olives, east of Jerusalem**. Then the LORD my God will come, and all the holy ones with him. The LORD will be king over the whole earth. On that day there will be one LORD, and his name the only name."

When's "that day?" That's the big question. Will it come? **God** says—good chance it's so. What happens before that and what happens after? Really hard to say—not as "pat" as some got it figured. Anything we can do to get the ground ready for him to put his resurrected feet down? Maybe. I'm going along with Paul—mostly Romans 11 (CJB).

Two fullnesses are here:

    1. Israel in its fullness (verse 12)
    2. Gentile world in its fullness (vs 25)

Israel's "stumbling" is bringing riches to the world. How much greater riches will Israel in its fullness bring the world! (12) It will be life from the dead! (15) **Of the Gentile fullness:** "stoniness, to a degree, has come upon Israel, until the Gentile world enters in its fullness; and. . . it is in this way that all Israel will be saved." (25, 26) All Israel will be saved by the Gentile world entering into its fullness—**whatever** that means. What if the **fullness of the Gentiles** means this? Enough Gentiles to fulfill their destiny of getting truly grafted into the cultivated olive tree of Israel (24). Aren't they already grafted in? Yes (17), but not in **fullness**—

Not **enough** branches grafted back in, receiving support from the holy root (16, 18), and the holy Jewish branches that are still on the cultivated olive tree (17).

Not a **fullness** of Gentiles respecting the whole loaf of Israel as being holy. (16).

Not a **fullness** of Gentiles yielding to **cultivated** olive tree grafting.

Not a **fullness** of Gentiles repenting of arrogance against Israel (20).

Not a **fullness** of Gentiles maintaining themselves in kindness toward Israel (22).

Not a **fullness** of Gentiles even **willing**, let alone **passionately praying and laboring,** for these natural Israeli branches to be grafted back into their own olive tree! (24)

Not a **fullness** of Gentiles who have repented of imagining they know more than they actually do about God's plan for Israel and the nations (25).

Not a **fullness** of Gentiles answering Paul's question like Paul did: "Isn't it that the Jews have stumbled with the result that they have **permanently fallen away? Heaven forbid! Quite the contrary!"** (11)

Not a **fullness** of Gentiles have heard their God-sent apostle's exhortation on what their God-required position is for Israel: "I exhort you, therefore, brothers, in view of God's mercies, to offer yourselves as a sacrifice, living and set apart for God. This will please him; it is the logical "Temple worship" for you. In other words, do not let yourselves be conformed to the standards of the 'olam hazeh (present world). Instead, keep letting yourselves be transformed by the renewing of your minds; so that you will know what God wants and will agree that what he wants (for Israel) is good, (what he wants for Israel is) satisfying and (what he wants for Israel is) **able to succeed."** (Romans 12: 1-3 CJB parentheses mine)

Not a **fullness** of Gentiles have heard: "For I am telling every single one of you, through the grace that has been given to me, not to have exaggerated ideas about your own (Gentile) importance. Instead, develop a sober estimate of yourself based on the standard which God has given to each of you, namely, trust." (Romans 12:3 CJB)

Not a **fullness** of Gentiles have heard regarding Israel **as a nation**: "God's free gifts and his calling are irrevocable. (Romans 11:29 CJB)

And **how many** Gentiles are close to their apostle's heartbeat for Israel? "My grief is so great, the pain in my heart so constant, that I could wish myself actually under God's curse and separated from the Messiah, if it would help my brothers, my own flesh and blood, the people of Israel!" (Romans 9:1-4a CJB) You see any fullness expressed in actions on that?

And who cries this cry? "Brothers, my heart's deepest desire and my prayer to God for Israel is for their salvation." (Romans 10:1 CJB)

How should Gentiles be feeling about the Jew in October 2002? "So don't be arrogant; on the contrary, **be terrified!**" (Romans 11:20 CJB)

Nothing even resembling a **fullness** of Gentiles **terrified** in church repentance over their centuries old, murderous arrogance against the Jews is in sight. How many Gentiles make a fullness? A remnant who will quit trying to stick their twig in Gentile ground to grow their **own** olive tree, and "go grafting" toward God's Israel-tree, willing to give up all their branch Sap into pulling the Son-shine down over Israel. **That's** fullness of the Gentiles. **In this manner** will all Israel be saved—**fullness of the Jews**. God will go forth over the nations from the Mount of Olives where Jesus used to hang out with his buddies.

CHAPTER 15

Miracles Going the Wrong Way

⟫•◦•⟪

Matthew 7:21ff again (THE MESSAGE):

"Knowing the correct password—saying 'Master, Master,' for instance—isn't going to get you anywhere with me. What is required is serious obedience—*doing* **what my Father wills**. I can see it now—at the Final Judgment thousands strutting up to me and saying, 'Master, we preached the Message, we bashed the demons, **our God-sponsored projects had everyone talking**.' And do you know what I am going to say? 'You missed the boat. **All you did was use me to make yourselves important.** You don't impress me one bit. **You're out of here**.'

Notice: "'Master, we preached the Message, we bashed the demons. . . .You're **out of here**.'" Other translations make it even tougher: "Didn't we prophesy in your name? Didn't we expel demons in your name? Didn't we perform many miracles in your name? Then he will tell them to their faces, 'I **never** knew you! **Get away from me, you workers of lawlessness!'"** (Stern's Complete Jewish Bible, CJB)

"Doing what my Father wills" struck me. Oh, I **do know**—just how far we all **do go**—to keep this verse from offending **anybody**, but what about this? I've just learned my Father wills to use restored Israel to reap the end-time harvest of nations. I **know** this, but I don't think "the church" that did **not** teach me **that** knows **that**. They wouldn't have kept it a secret. I've seen miracles; I've received miracles; I need **more** miracles. Now I'm asking, "How much does 'doing what my Father wills' have to do with us getting more miracles?" See how much sense this makes: if Father wills that he get back Israel as his wife (the prophets absolutely heard him saying that), and I am not (and the church is not) **doing** what Father wills in the matter, could that create a miracle power problem? "What is required is **serious** obedience—**doing** what my Father wills."

Jesus says to people who have prophesied, cast out demons, and performed miracles: **"You missed the boat."** What's the boat? Is it **using miracle power** to birth the kingdom of God **in Israel?** Check this out: "All you did was **use** me (**and my miracle power**) to make **yourselves** (your churches, your ministries, your programs and agendas) important." How else could they have used God to make themselves important, if they weren't promoting their own plans? No wonder they didn't impress him: "You don't impress me one bit. **"You're out of here."** After they used all that power, he threw 'em out! Is Yeshua equally unimpressed with Gentile church hulla-baal-u?

Take CJBs version: "I never knew you! Get away from me, you workers of lawlessness!" (If **that's** not missing the boat. . . .) "Lawlessness" is no-law, no serious obedience to Father-law, or Father's will. "You missed the boat," you missed the plan. You're stranded—on land, out on desert sand, and the boat's gone. Bet the boatload is bound for Israel where the remnant of the church joins the remnant of Israel to give serious obedience to Father's will that his feet stand on the Mount of Olives, that his law of the Spirit of life flow and blow from Israel in her destiny, and out through all the nations. Serious obedience to **Father's** will about Israel and the Jews is bound to help restore full deliverance power to his **true** hurting church **in order for the church to be his instrument in getting Israel delivered to their destiny.**

Here's an allegory: Suppose **you** were God? You love your family; you miss them. You want them back home with you for the Holy Season. You gave First Gentile Church your family bus, The Zion Express (call it "The X") and sent for your family. They receive The X because it's a cool way to travel. Your worldwide House hook-up keeps The X fueled and humming with miracle energy. You're really lonesome for your family. The X carries an unlimited supply of regenerating Power-Paks that strap on to each passenger; each can fully access your own Power. You're getting excited about hugging all your family.

The X works heavenly—the bus, Power supply, and Power-Paks. Gentile workers "win souls," welcome them into The X, and pass out the Power-Paks. You're watching through your House hookup. This is good, more help that's needed to go after your family. You're smiling as the driver fires up The X, and heads for the Freeway. In all the buzz aboard the bus, Smitty makes a wrong turn—heads The X **away** from your family.

Oh no! You stand up and call to 'em, but you can't get their attention. You **turn up** their Power so they can hear you better. Smitty's not listening; he's carried away, "Wow man, **feel** that **Power**." He floorboards it, and you watch The X go barreling down the Freeway—**on the wrong side**, courting a head-on collision. You don't want anyone hurt; you don't want 'em delayed. What to do? You turn up miracle Power all through the bus to get their attention; **no** one is paying any. They're gripped with "ridingitis," while you're gripped with pain. Your heart aches and throbs; you sob online, but nobody hears your crying; they aren't listening. They're riding high-wrong-and-handsome—sold on themselves. **Nobody** feels your heartache; by now, they're too far away—and headed full speed **farther** away—away from you, away from your family. **Nobody** sees the tears sparkling golden crystal rivers down your face; they aren't looking. They're on a party roll—in the hottest church program bus on the planet. They don't need to hear you now. They've got the power and they can handle it **themselves**.

What would you do? Would you give them **more** power to take them **further** from your family, and from you, from their destiny, from your plan for the planet? Would **you** do more healing and miracles for them to **use** you to make **themselves** more important, more powerful, more prestigious, more comfortable—to give them bigger bragging rights to speed them into an even **more** dangerous crash? **"All you did was use me to make yourselves important."** What **would** you do—if you were God?

CHAPTER 16

"Voodoo"

≈≫•○•≪≈

Copyright © 2002, Daniel Gray
(Used by permission)

1. Don't need to go to Africa to see those natives
   dance.
   Don't need to go to Haiti to be put in a trance.
   Don't need to go to New Orleans to see the
   Mardi Gras
   Cause you can find the devil's touch right there
   where you are.

2. While kids are in rebellion and salesmen they
   do lie
   Wives look right at their husbands and give the
   evil eye.
   I don't know what to do about this witchcraft
   that I see.
   Everyone I know keeps putting voodoo on me.

(chorus)

Everyone I know keeps putting voodoo on me.
Everywhere I go that twisted wicker I see.
I look for truth because the truth sets me free. But everyone I know keeps putting voodoo on me.

3.   I went down to the crossroads and I made myself a deal.

Really got my life messed up; this devil cat is real.

So then I got religion 'cause I needed to be free

But everyone I know keeps putting voodoo on me.

4.   The mother of my children I went and got her vexed.

Her anger it was justified so now my life is hexed.

She calls me on the telephone to give me misery.

Everyone I know keeps putting voodoo on me.

5.   I studied really hard to find the secrets to life.

Made necessary changes, better habits, better wife.

I told it to the world because I wanted them to see

But everyone I know keeps putting voodoo on me.

6.   My children they need gasoline; they need them Nike shoes

They need them things I can't afford just playing Christian Blues.

So I go down to work each day to end my poverty

But even at my job they're putting voodoo on

me.

7.   I went down to the churches and I said, "We've been deceived."
They didn't like my message so I finally had to leave.
I hob-nobbed with apostles and the folks in prophecy
But even in the church they're putting voodoo on me.

8.   So now I look for Jesus 'cause I know he never lies.
I'm hoping somehow I can find the answer to my cries.
I feel just like Zaccheus; I'm stuck up in a tree
'Cause everyone I know keeps putting voodoo on me.

9.   Lies, manipulations, being in control.
One message coming from your mouth, another in your soul.
Yes is no and no is yes and that's no way to be.
You get your way but you been putting voodoo on me.

10.   God's cards are on the table; he doesn't need a trick
But charismatic witchcraft just makes the whole church sick.
The Holy Spirit tells the truth I hope that you agree
Cause everyone I know's been putting voodoo on me.

(chorus)
Everyone I know's been putting voodoo on me.

Everywhere I go that twisted wicker I see.
I look for truth because the truth sets me free.
But everyone I know keeps putting voodoo on me.

Part Four: WARNING! Woman Stuff Ahead—Read at Your Own Risk!

———»·0·«———

G od's whole thing about marriage is spiritual intimacy. He uses marriage to picture for us how tender and full his love is for Israel, (and all who are his). We cannot think **primarily** of the physical. God is Spirit. He reveals Himself **to** physical, **in** physical, and **through** physical, but he is Spirit. We see here that God had a wife **in** a physical people, Israel. He was married to Israel. If Israel is his wife, then he's revealing a male likeness. One preacher was quoted, "I believe God is 100 percent male." Fine—as long as we also understand that God is 100 percent female. Right? (**Didn't** you read the warning sign!) Or, should we say, "God is 81 percent Father and 19 percent Son? Oops, what about Spirit? Let's see: three into one hundred is— 33 and a third!" **Not** Spirit-directed thinking. God is one, not one divided by three.) God is male; God is female. He can **do** that—he's **God**. Israel is also spoken of as God's son, which would make God Israel's Father. So, he's Israel's husband—and— father? Yep. But he said he was Israel's Husband-Maker. I know. He's her Creator too. Go figure—God's way—with the mind of Christ. See, we have to go with God's kind of thinking. He also sounds like Israel's Mother in a few places. Don't worry—hey—**God** can handle it! (But can you?) He's not afraid of losing his macho image. So, remember. When I speak of God as Family, I'm **not** talking **primarily** physical. It is **critical** that you remember this.

CHAPTER 17

"Clump" Change

L et's take one giant step for mankind here—put on our eagle wings and go high for a **wide** overview. Then, we'll do the woman stuff.

I can't find in the Book where God says, "My name is 'Used to Be,' or "Gonna Be." If he is "I AM" today, what is he tomorrow? Is he "I AM" tomorrow—when tomorrow's not even here yet? What was he yesterday? Was he "I AM" yesterday? And he's "I AM" tomorrow? Funny talk? If he is "I AM" tomorrow and I am **in** "I AM" today, how come I'm not **already** in "I AM" tomorrow—and already in tomorrow? The eternal realm is fluid like that—ever flowing, ever changing. God's ready already—to do stuff **today**—not just "tomorrow." I'm convinced of it. **I'm** the one needing to get with it—needing to open up to **I Am** right here where I **now** am. Our old no-anointed nature panics at the thought of change, but I remember Adonica

Howard-Browne's warning: "**Constant** change is here to **stay**." I'm challenged to change by checking my "what ifs." So I ask myself:

♦ **What if** "The earth is the Lords and all it contains, the world and those who dwell in it" (Psalm 24:1).

♦ **What if** God **keeps** the earth?

♦ **What if** God does not grab off all the good folk and run off to heaven with them?

♦ **What if** he does not tuck-tail and leave the earth for the devil and the bad guys?

♦ **What if** God's not biting his nails 'till he can snatch you up out of "this old wicked world" to set you softly into all the comforts of heaven?

♦ **What if** getting you to a greater comfort zone is not #1 on God's priority list?

♦ **What if** God decides to keep the earth—forever? **What if** he decided before he ever created it that he had no intention of abandoning his creation to Satan?

♦ **What if** God's not looking forward to the day when he can say to the devil from his high and safe place, "Goody, goody. I got away from you?"

♦ **What if** God has not the tee-niniest notion—like it never **once** crossed his mind to have a people eager to run off to heaven to escape the devil so **they** could say, "Goody, goody—didn't get **me**?"

♦ **What if**—all these things? Would you have to adjust any of your beliefs? How would your theology fare? Could your present thought routes stand the strain?

♦ **What if** God's heart was set, not on having a

run-off-to-hide people, but rather set on having a people walking around on earth, praising him and worshiping him? **What if** God scheduled that kind of movement to go over all the earth, taking it back for him as they went? Would you want to sign on?

♦ **What if** this movement was headed all the way back to where God started out so God could enjoy seeing Satan ground into the very grit he slithered on to trick Eve? How would you deal with that— if that were God's pleasure?

♦ **What if** God was just doing a spiritual swing-by to pick up you and your family on his way back into Jerusalem?

♦ **What if** he did **not** have in mind hanging out with you just so your church would be "cool?"

♦ **What if** he had in mind for you to **serve** him and **his** dream? And he wanted to give you a chance to be in **his** plan? He's dropping by to give you one chance to go with him. He's got an agenda. He's on a mission. He can't hang around to change your diddies and powder your booty forever, but he **does** want you to be with him. Would you go with him? Would you accept the **change** required? Left up to you. Who would care for your pets? I don't know. What would happen to your baby pet-beliefs? You have to travel really light—and, you don't have forty forevers to make up your mind. "Time's short," he says, "I'm giving you one shot at it. Come on—seize the moment!"

♦ **What if**—well, let's just leap way out on this

one: **What if God's really on his way to get the Jews** and he's offering to let you go along? He needs your cooperation. Too tough to take? Going after **Israel**? Kind of a slap in the face, is it? Would you have this, uh—you know, "Israel problem? "Israel's in the past," or "Israel's in the future," or, "Don't bother me about Israel" problem?

♦ **What if** all these outpourings over the world are lightning bolts (See Ezekiel 1:14) that clear out clean "foot-spots"—places where Ancient of Days can step on the land without killing every living thing **in** the land as he walks the nations on his way back to Jerusalem?

♦ **What if** he's headed up to Jerusalem for the feast again? Except this time it's the marriage feast of the Lamb? Would you want to go along with him? Yes? No? Could you still sing, "Yea Lord, I embrace your move. Yea, Lord, I embrace your love?"

♦ **What if** the fullness of the Gentiles is upon us and we **must** be **truly love-grafted** into the Israel-nation olive tree—not just **debate theology**? When God gets enough Gentiles to set-in the graft, the "nations" **will be** grafted in. The old tree will take on new life through the Yeshua graft, and the broken off Jewish branches will come for their grafting **back** in. So shall all Israel be saved.

♦ **What if** it's "One Shepherd, one flock" time? Are you saying, "Well, I don't know about that?" But **What if** you've just been looking at your little

Gentile branch and never once glanced up to notice God has a whole olive grove back in Hebrew country?

♦ **What if**, in this old olive grove in Israel, God's after producing enough oil to light the Yeshua Torch for the planet, making it shine in creativity to yield a new, globe-glistening earth under the new heaven? You do know the Bible **promises** this? A new heaven and a new earth? John already saw it. You say, "Yeah, but that's way off in the future?" Who says? What does "I AM" say? John started off saying these were things that would shortly come to pass. (Revelation 1) John didn't say it was way off in the future—even back then.

♦ **What if**, all this time, God has been searching for a group of people that would storm through the principalities and powers of darkness in the name of Jesus to claim what is already at hand? Possess what already has come down from heaven?

♦ **What if** Father hasn't been able to find a group of believers to really believe—that the invisible world is real—that it can be faith-entered by calling those things that be not as though they already existed?

♦ **What if** calling those things that are invisible as if they were already visible **enables** Father to release creativity **in earth** to reproduce what's already done in heaven?

♦ **What if** God, who calls those things that do not exist as though they already exist—what if he sees and says, "I've got some kids out there that are talking like me. They want to be like me. Let me see what they're saying. If they're talking like me, get out there, heavenly creatures and take care of these kids. Make 'em like me."

♦ **What if** these Gentile churches all come together to be living parts of a living body, living bones brought alive in their own dry bone valleys? One new Gentile fullness, quivering with resurrection life, **pointed at Israel for grafting?**

♦ **What if** these many living body parts become the living true Vine of Yeshua's kingdom, spreading rapidly to swallow up the whole earth into Father's purpose **back in Israel?**

♦ **What if** John really did see New Jerusalem coming down from God out of heaven?

♦ **What if** New Jerusalem **is** here and available, but religion has blinded our minds to what **we already have**, and kept us living in a visible-world stupor? A bitter, bitter pill to swallow. Enough to give you the "heebie-geebies!" Enough to make you say, "Have I been in a drugged out, dragon coma, sleeping my way into oblivion? I thought I was just killing time 'til the second coming rapture. Have I been missing something here?"

♦ **What if** you could stand one or two more of these?

♦ **What if** this Gentile fullness of a quivering resurrected Yeshua falls into Father's dream? Joseph was a dreamer. He dreamed it, but it did happen. He dreamed about wheat clumps bowing down, didn't he? Growing up on the farm, I remember wind blowing to clump lots of stalks all into one clump, leaning all into each other.

♦ **What if** there were clumps formed by Ezekiel's whirlwinds out of heaven, and these clumps were the re-forming of a people in a new earth to fit the pattern in a new heaven? Now all are in the one field, no more divisive clumps, no denominational clumps—no clumps a-tall. All clumps clumped together by the Lord of all clumps, using his Holy Breath.

♦ **What if** one of these clumps was a group of farmers that formed a co-op? They contract with the head Clumper to produce all the food needed in the new earth. (Like in Almalonga, Guatamala where the whole city was transformed.)

♦ **What if** another clump was a group of Jesus folk with God given abilities in the health care field? Their goal: deliver the mercy of Father to mankind through medical care and treatment—give the mercy of our Father to the whole hurting world.

♦ **What if** another clump was a group with building abilities whose goal was to let Yeshua use them to provide housing—homes, churches, buildings for the whole new creation?

♦ **What if** you got a vision that the kingdoms of this world could actually become the kingdoms of our Lord and his Anointed? Not just a pipe dream off out yonder in the foggy, pie-in-the-sky future—after "the" rapture, but this thing could actually happen right here in Hometowns, USA and **rupture** Satan's roosting place?

♦ **What if** this clumping was working right now,

spreading out, undetectable, crawling like yeast through the whole creation?—undercover, well hidden, like moles underground—like a thief in the night? The yeast rising to possess and take over the clumps of this world and make them the clumps of our Lord, the Head Clumper.

♦ **What if** this Captain Clumper has as his sponsoring banker-backer in this project his Daddy, the **Owner-Creator** of the whole field and all clumps everywhere? He holds all copyrights, all patents.

♦ **What if** Cap'n Clumper and Creator are buried in this project together, head over heel? Who could spoil the project? Who could stop the spread? Pull off a corporate takeover? Know of anyone who could buy 'em out?

♦ **What if** (up-close and personal now) "Joe" said no? Think the whole thing would die? Would the clumping stop? Would the whole project shut down? All the clumps wither and die? Or would other parts in Joe's clump get Joe's share? Joe said no—said, "I just don't believe in all that scary, prophetic stuff." Tough. What just changed? **Nothing!** Except Joe's chance to change and get in on it. That's **all**. Think about it.

♦ **What if** some long-established, prestigious religious structure refused the clumping? Oh! **surely** heaven would shudder, shake, and shut the whole thing down—and apologize profusely on "bended clouds!" You think? Who do you figure would last longer? That earthly powerful, unclumped religious empire, or the clumps of the heavenly Clumper-Creator?—though his clumps **appeared** weak, nameless, and faceless?

♦ **What if** the Chief Clumper raised up Nameless Faceless for his very own corporate quarters? Didn't ask a living soul. Didn't take an opinion poll. Didn't do a house to house. Didn't seek anybody's say. He just reared back on his throne and—**bam!** Burning yeast-fire of God in Nameless Faceless, in a simple little setting of love seekers.

♦ **What if** God gushes gas on the group's little love flame? He got tired of waiting. **Change** was going way too slow. He said, "Let all the religions **keep** their famous religious stuff—off out there to the side for now. I'll just hang out here with Nameless Faceless. They don't have anything more important to do than serve me in worship. Religious Famous can do as he pleases; **I'll** do as **I** please. I'll fan love's fire and push my regenerating process. I'm ready now for a new earth on the pattern of the new heaven for my Son. He deserves it now. Right here in Nameless Faceless, I'll set up my Gentile Church Processing Plant. I'll see how many will follow me when I fan into the next blaze—when they see I've already **come out** of heaven, and **headed for** Jerusalem to sound the final shofar blast to take care of kingdom-**on-earth** business. What do you think, Elijah? How many? John? How many? "Joe, Jim, Joan, or Jane?" How many?

What if: In the last days the mountain of the LORD'S temple will be established as chief (clump) among the mountains; it will be raised above the hills, and peoples will stream to it (to become one clump).

"2   **Many nations** will come and say, "**Come, let us go up** to the mountain of the LORD, **to the house of the God of Jacob.** He will teach us his ways, so that we may walk in his paths." The law will go out **from Zion,** the word of the LORD **from Jerusalem.**

3   "He will judge between many peoples and will settle disputes for strong nations far and wide.

They will beat their swords into plowshares and their spears into pruning hooks.

Nation will not take up sword against nation, **nor will they train for war anymore.**

4   Every man will sit under his own vine and under his own fig tree, and **no one will make them afraid**, for the LORD Almighty has spoken.

5"All the nations may walk in the name of their gods; we will walk in the name of the LORD our God for ever and ever. 6"In that day," declares the LORD, "**I will gather the lame (hey that's me!)**; I will assemble the exiles and those I have brought to grief.

7   "**I will make the lame a remnant (me again!)**, those driven away **a strong nation.**

The LORD will rule over them **in Mount**

Zion, from that day and forever.

8 As for you, O watchtower of the flock, O stronghold of the Daughter of Zion, **the former dominion will be restored to you; <u>kingship</u> will come to the Daughter of Jerusalem."**

9 "Why do you now cry aloud—have you no king? Has your counselor perished, that pain seizes you like that of a woman in labor? 10Writhe in agony, O Daughter of Zion, **like a woman in labor,** for now you must leave the city to camp in the open field. **You will go to Babylon; there you will be rescued. There the LORD will redeem you** out of the hand of your enemies.

11 "But now many nations are gathered against you. They say, "Let her be defiled, let our eyes gloat over Zion!"

12 "**<u>But</u> they do not know** the thoughts of the LORD;

they do not understand his plan, he who **gathers them like sheaves** to the threshing floor.

13 "**<u>Rise and thresh, O Daughter of Zion,</u> for I will give you** horns of iron; **I will give you** hoofs of bronze, and **you** will break to pieces many nations." **You** will devote their ill-gotten gains to the LORD, their wealth to the Lord of all the earth. **(Micah 4)**

CHAPTER 18

Contractions (Not an English Class— The Other Kind)

--->=·0·=<---

W here do they come from? Really. They tend to show up connected with pregnancy when it gets close to **"the time"** (words to make a husband tremble!) Didn't you ever wonder where they come from? I mean, the woman's doing just fine, chattering away, when—**suddenly**, right in the middle of a sentence, **Oh! Ho-o-o-o-o-oh-h-h!** and it's **on**, buddy. She's **gone**. No warning. **"They"** just come out o' nowhere and **hit**. **Love** to catch you off guard—just—**there they are—bang!** Like, right out of thin air. (Ever notice? Nothing comes out of **thick** air.) Since contractions come out of nowhere, I figure, they're lurking out there somewhere in the shadows, hiding in that thin air. Said to myself,

"That begs investigation." Let's start where I like to start—with the Bible.

Jeremiah 30 (NRSV) "[5]Thus says the LORD: We have heard **a cry of panic, of terror, and no peace.** [6]Ask now, and see, **can a man bear a child? Why then** do I see **every man** with his hands on his loins **like a woman in labor?** Why has every face turned pale? [7]Alas! that day is so great, there is none like it; it is a time of distress for **Jacob**; yet he shall be rescued from it."

That's bad, men (or is it?); means we get 'em too. Not sure how much that helped our cause. There's not only more than one contraction; there's more than one **kind** of 'em—if men get hit too. Maybe better luck in the New Testament? Looking for clues here.

Galatians 4:19, "My little children, for whom I am again **in the pain of childbirth** until Christ is **formed** in you." Now we have a double challenge. Here's Paul, a **man**, saying he's been hit—plus, Christ was being formed **in** these people—and you know what's eventually going to happen if Christ is being formed **in** them, right? For Christ to come **out?** What? These folk are in the danger zone too. Contractions are lurking out there for 'em—**somewhere!** Just waiting to come out of thin air. It's getting bad, huh? They **are** out there—you agree? Aliens maybe? More investigation required: Here's a pregnant woman in Revelations 12. Whoa! This woman's very pregnant and "it's time."

"[1]A great and wondrous sign appeared in heaven: a woman clothed with the sun, with the moon under her feet and a crown of twelve stars on her head. ²She was **pregnant and cried out in pain (contractions, no doubt)** as she was **about to give birth.** ⁵**She gave birth** to a son, a male child, who will rule all the nations with an iron scepter. And her child was **snatched up** to God and to his throne. ⁶The woman fled into the desert to a place prepared for her by God, where she might **be taken care of** for 1,260 days."

Hmm. Let's see one more case—this one with a **long** gestation period—**5160 months!** That's long. It's back in the Old Testament (Exodus, chapters 7-14), and her name is Israel. She went through **so many** contractions! Whew! I finally just picked the top 10. They were so hard that the Bible calls them plagues—**heavy** contractions—had to be, I guess, since this was to birth out a whole nation. And, look at that birth canal! This baby nation was coming through the canal that stretched all the way across the Red Sea—longest birth canal I've read about till I found this woman in the Rev 12 delivery room. You can study it there and help with the investigation. I found that the Husband-Doctor God "broke her water" and induced labor to get her out of the womb of Egypt. Then he pulled the baby out, all the way across the sea with water all around 'em. Worst afterbirth I ever heard of though. Oh my! Leftover stuff **everywhere**—all out in the sea, all over the beach—**yucky**! It was **bad**—blood all over **everything**—messy, messy, **messy!** But the baby made it through, and the nation got squalling.

Well "Watson," we didn't solve the contractions

mystery. I can tell this will be one of those long-running investigations. Keep up with the clues. The woman in Rev 12 who's about to give birth is worthy of a stakeout. (Keep tabs on the one in Revelation 17 too.)

CHAPTER 19

God as Husband—God as Wife (Uch-oh! Now We've Done it!)

———⟫•⟪———

"**P**op" sat there in "Heart and Pen" writing class, listening to Mark Murphree call the roll. He had **not** planned to go back to school—just wanted to enjoy visiting the International House of Prayer (IHOP). "Yep," he said to himself, "Just like I figured—oldest in the class—probably oldest ol' coot ever to take his first formal writing class." He thought about the bumper sticker "If you can't run with the big dogs, stay on the porch." He pined for his porch—on the cabin—on the lake—where the sun made the water sparkle like diamonds before it settled down through the trees—where Mama Doe brought her twin babies into the yard to show 'em off—where the squirrels ran headfirst down the tree trunk and stopped to visit with you ten feet away—where the rabbits ran and the wild geese flocked as they pleased—where "Shugah" had nothing more important to do than share it all with him. He was pining away when Mark called his name—"Gross!" "Here." Pop was making it—one class at a time. Then, one day Mark talked "paradigm"—"Bridal paradigm."

Say, "Bridal paradigm." "Bridal **what**?" I **know**. I didn't like the word either, but seems it's a growing thing, here to stay. It's used by a lot by worshippers, especially here at IHOP Kansas City. Song of Solomon (SOS) is used a lot to reveal Christ as the bridegroom and the church as his bride. I'm on record, saying, "Song of Solomon is not in the Bible **primarily** to paint a picture of Christ and the church." (Uch-oh!) So I understand people who struggle with what Mike Bickle and "Friends of the Bridegroom" at IHOP are doing here 24/7. But forget Song of Solomon—just for a minute. Here's what I'd like to do: (1) Define "bridal paradigm." (2) Take you to Scripture **outside** Song of Solomon to show you that bridal paradigm is God-induced, love labor for a thought-system shift, and (3) Help you see that bridal paradigm does not live or die on SOS—that it is **so** old as to **predate** civilization. In doing this, we'll see why Eve was "brought forth," Who "Us" is in "Let us make man," and who "Wisdom" is in Proverbs. By time we finish, you'll be thinking fresh thoughts about bridal paradigm (and hopefully, **not** hunting the phone to call the heresy squad).

Lou Engle offers a simple definition of "paradigm": "A paradigm is a box that holds together similar ideological, social, and spiritual views." (*KAIROS*, July-Sept 2002, "God The Paradigm Buster," page 24.) The **bridal** paradigm, therefore, is a box that holds together similar ideological, social, and spiritual **bridal** views.

Genesis 1:26-27 (CJB) to answer the question, "Why was Eve brought forth from inside Adam, and **not** made out of dirt like Adam?" "Then God said, 'Let us make humankind in our **image**, in the **likeness** of ourselves . . .' So God created humankind in his own **image**; in the **image** of God he created him; male **and female** he created them."

Now Genesis 2:21-25 (CJB):

"Then God caused a deep sleep to fall upon the person; and while he was sleeping, he took one of his ribs and closed up the place from which he took it with flesh. The rib which ADONAI, God, **had taken from the person, he made a woman-person**; and he brought her to the man-person. The man-person said, 'At last! This is bone from **my** bones and flesh from **my** flesh. She is to be called woman . . ., because she was **taken out of man** . . . .' This is why a man is to leave his father and mother and stick with his wife, and they are to be **one flesh**. . . ."

Notice that God set out to create humankind in "our **image**," and in "our **likeness.**" Eve was "brought forth" out of Adam because there was an **image** and a **likeness** in God that required her to "come forth" in this manner for there to be **exact** reproduction of image and likeness.

Proverbs 8:22-9:6 (CJB) calls up wisdom. Now, who is "wisdom"? Is wisdom part of "us?" (Note: For "wisdom" in this passage, the Greek Septuagint uses the Greek word, "sophia." I use Sophia, with **no deliberate intent** to connect or disconnect with theological views in print about "Sophia.") If you said, "Wisdom is Jesus," then you are right: "He (Messiah) has become wisdom for us." (1 Cor 1:30). True. I also note: "The Lord (Messiah) **is the Spirit.**" (2 Cor 3:17) Question: **How** did Jesus "become wisdom for us?" **How** was Yeshua **made** wisdom for us? Was it not by the Spirit? Is Jesus not the Word? Was not the Word **in the beginning**? Did not Abba speak Word **by** his Spirit and create all that was created through Word? Was it not his Spirit who **carried** Word in order to bring forth Father's creation? Does not Father still work this way? Was it not the Spirit, one with Word-Jesus, that made Jesus wisdom? Was Spirit made Wisdom in order to make Jesus wisdom—or did Spirit just mechanically tote wisdom in a stork basket or something? I'm seeing God's Spirit, one with Father, becoming Wisdom of Father and showing Son to be one with Father—Spirit being one with Son and Father—Carrier of "the Lord who is that Spirit," Carrier-Spirit of Word-Jesus for Creator-Father God.

Wisdom is the one talking here. Context consciousness is required **all the way to the end of the passage.**

"ADONAI made me **as** the beginning of his way, The **first** of his **ancient** works. I was appointed

before the world.

(Note break: NIV has 8:22, 23 like this: "The LORD **brought me forth** as the **first** of his works,— (First note says, "or, **way**, or **dominion**. Second one says, "The LORD **possessed** me at the beginning of his work," or, "The LORD **brought me forth** at the beginning of his work); before his deeds of old; I was appointed– (Note says "or, **fashioned**) from eternity ..." So an acceptable, scholarly translation is: "The LORD **possessed** me at the beginning of his work; before his deeds of old, I was **fashioned from eternity**.")

"**Before** the start, **before** the earth's beginnings.

When **<u>I was brought forth</u>**, there were no ocean depths, No springs brimming with water.

<u>I was brought forth</u> before the hills,

Before the mountains had settled in place;

He had **not yet** made the earth, the fields, or even the earth's first grains of dust.

When he established **the heavens, I was there...**

(So the LORD **possessed** Sophia from **eternity** and **brought her forth** to help in creation.)

<u>"I was with him</u> as someone he could trust.

For me, every day was pure delight, as I played in his presence **all the time**,

Playing everywhere on his earth, and **<u>delighting</u> to be with humankind.**

(Note break: NIV has "Then **I was the craftsman at his side**. I was **filled with delight day after day, rejoicing** always in his presence, **rejoicing** in his **whole** world and **delighting in mankind**." Let's review: The LORD **possessed** Sophia from **eternity**

and **brought her forth** to help in creation—to be a "fellow-craftsman," or co-Creator in his **whole** world.)

"Therefore, **children**, listen to me…for he who finds me finds life

And obtains the favor of ADONAI . . .

Wisdom has built **herself** a house; **she** has carved her seven pillars.

She has prepared **her** food, spiced **her** wine, and **she** has set **her** table.

She has sent out **her** young girls (with invitations);

She calls **from the heights of the city**, 'Whoever is unsure of himself, turn in here!'

To someone weak-willed **she** says, **'Come and eat my food! Drink the wine I have mixed.**

Don't stay unsure of yourself, but **live**! Walk in the way of understanding!'

I see "Sophia" as the female GodMate—the female working of the Godhood. I think the **likeness** and **image** of God is the likeness and image of Adam (male) and Eve (female) in the Garden— when God got through **doing** what **God said** he was going to do. I mean, did God lie? Or, did God do what he said he was going to do? **That** question has to be answered **first**. I say, "**Of course** God did what he said he was going to do! Is God a man, that he should lie? That image and likeness God created after his own image and likeness includes male and female. Therefore, there is in God:

- ♦ God-Male
- ♦ God-Female.

God-Female can be God-Wisdom, same as God-Male (Father-Son) can be God-Wisdom." Make sense? It really **needs** to! I freak at the thought of **any** kind of birthing going on, old **or** new, without **female** participation and involvement. A "males only" birthing? Now, **that's** weird! You don't think that's weird? Come on now—you know that's ("funny") weird. It just doesn't happen. I mean—human or animal—a **real** birth calls to mind—what? **Female**! True? Or, **not**? Is my thinking leaking? If **males** giving birth **without** a female is not weird to you. . .

Come on—time to let God out of the "male-box" 'fore he **blasts** out. He almost **has** a'ready. Look around. Good-o-boy clubs are coming down. Let's continue. Who is "us?" If "Sophia" is female GodMate, "us" is the GodMate-Family— Father-Mother-Son. Then God is Family, like he imaged in creation. Invisible, yes, but God is Family. From this heaven-side, **invisible** Family, "us" decided to create a reflection of Himself—an earth-side **visible** family. **"Us"** did precisely what **"us" said "us" was going to do.** I **believe** that about "us"—that "They" are **like** that—"They" say it, and "They" **do** it.

Summing up: Sophia was "brought forth," to be **with,** and work **alongside** Abba in his work of creation. Eve was "brought forth" from inside Adam to be a helper alongside Adam in his work—according to God's **image** and **likeness**. Listen to Sophia speaking to her **children;** think about Spirit workings in other Scriptures. Feel Abba's heartbeat for his children in Wisdom's cry. Notice language of new Jerusalem and the bridal supper—even invitations going out.

Then I ask, "Did Paul get into bridal paradigm stuff?" Answer: "the Jerusalem above **is our mother**." (See Galatians 4:26)

Anything from Apostle of love, John? Revelations 21 (NKJV), "**2**I saw the Holy City, the new Jerusalem, **coming down** out of heaven **from God**, prepared as **a bride** beautifully **dressed for her husband**. **3**And I heard a loud voice from the throne saying, "**Now** the dwelling of **God** is with **men**, and he will **live with them** . . . **God himself will be with them**. . . . **the old order of things** has passed away."

What's going **on**? God's getting his Garden **back in earth**. The **Holy** City is a **woman <u>coming down</u>** out of heaven **from God**—God extended ("brought forth"). Once this beautifully "dressed for her husband" **Bride**-City settled down out of heaven, John wrote, "**Now <u>God</u>** lives here." God lives here **with the same Wife he had in the first Garden. He brought Her forth then; he brings Her forth now.** (Been **doing** it ever since Eden!) The old order of things is **out**; heaven's order is back **in**—**no** options. God's heart-order cries, "Bride"; our head-order screams, "Program." Our gearbox is busted; our paradigm bridal-ly bankrupt. God's all **right**—we're all wrong.

Picking up again with verse 9: "Come, **I will show you the bride, the Lamb's wife**." **10**And he carried me away **in the Spirit** to a great and high mountain, and showed me the great city, the holy

Jerusalem, **descending <u>out of</u> heaven from God**, **¹¹having the glory of God**. <u>Her</u> light was like a most precious stone . . . . **she** had a great and high wall . . . . , <u>its</u> gates (**Note Pause**: I found no difference in this Greek translated "its" and the "her" of **"her** light" just before. Why did translators switch pronouns—**away** from feminine? [**Couldn't** have been gender prejudice! Shame, shame, "Good ol' boys."] Let's stay feminine. Put "she" for "it," etc. and keep going. Keep the Woman in sight and compare her with Sophia in Proverbs 8:22-9:6. We need this understanding also for Revelation 12; there, with dragon breath in her face, the woman's in hard labor to **give birth** to the new order in earth.)

♦ So it's **her** gates, and **her** wall.
♦ The city is laid out as a square; **her** length is as great as **her** breadth.
♦ **Her** length, breadth, and height are equal. ¹⁷Then he measured **her** wall.
♦ The construction of **her** wall
♦ The Lord God Almighty and the Lamb are **her** temple.
♦ The nations of those who are saved shall walk in **her** light,
♦ The kings of the earth bring their glory and honor into **her**.
♦ **Her** gates shall not be shut.
♦ They shall bring the glory and the honor of the nations into **her**.
♦ But there shall by no means enter **her** anything that defiles."

Compare this city with Sophia's house. What do

you think?

Just a mention of two other Scriptures:

1. "The Spirit of God **hovered** over the surface of the water (**birthing** creation)." (Genesis 1:2. Strong on "hovered": "to **brood** . . . flutter") On the farm, we had brood mares, brood sows, and fluttering, "setting" (brooding) chickens—**All** females—all **brooding** to **birth**. Not a waiting-to-birth stud, boar or rooster in the bunch.

2. The angel answered, "The Holy Spirit will **come upon you**, <u>and</u> the power of the Most High (Mother and Father working) will overshadow you. So the holy one **to be born** will be called the Son of God." (Luke 1:35) Sophia "carried" Seed to the womb and, in Mary's body, "carried" Jesus to **birthing**. (Now, she puts Seed in believer's spirit for the new birth.)

This is all bridal paradigm with no mention of Song of Solomon. Where's The Song's place? Is it an allegory? That's a "Yes, but" (from what revelation I've received). It's **better** than allegory. Listen. The Garden is being kept in Father. He wants it back out in earth. Jesus **will** get us to **Father** intimacy in Eden-Jerusalem. It is **written**, "At that day you will know (experience) that **I am in My Father, and you in Me**, and I in you." (John 14:20 NKJV) How will Yeshua do it? "And I **in** you." He's **in** us to **take** us into Father, the final Frontier. We can live in the bridal paradigm now—at **some** level—while Sophia "allures" us deeper. Remember: "(he) gives life to

160

the dead and calls things that are not as though they were." (Romans 4:17) Yeshua licensed us to talk like Papa. There is no time—therefore no time **limits**—in faith.

Yeshua is the **Way** into Father. Once he delivers us into Abba—here **in earth**, Abba and Mama live in us. (Don't leave me now.) Let's say Jesus delivers a "Sam" and a "Suzy" into Father by the Spirit. Father then lives in Sam and Suzy. In Abba's plan, Sam and Suzy become one flesh so God can love God as Sam and Suzy love each other. God loves God in them. As they love each other, they're loving God. What Abba takes his liberty to do is to create the males in his likeness and image, while creating the females in Sophia's likeness and image. Abba and Mama are then revealed in the earth through their creation as the ultimate, supreme, Super-Lover. They love each Other **in**, and out **through** Sam and Suzy (Solomon and the Shulamite, Christ and the church, Abba and Israel).

This is the **ultimate love relationship. It yearns and burns for "The Song of all Love Songs."** GodMates live **in** and **among** flesh and blood humankind—Abba's dream being **love-lived** out through their created beings. These **new-birthed** creatures, Sam and Suzy, have merged, meshed and melted—fiber, bone and being into God **Oneness**—back into **his** image and his likeness. (The inclusive "his" is "her" and Seed-Word, who are One with him.) Oneness is **all** intimacy, but **all** intimacy is not oneness. There are degree levels of intimacy. **Here** in **Abba** intimacy of **husband and wife in earth** is where "The Song" **ultimately** belongs forever—an allegory being **lived out** in meshed (heaven-earth) marriages—personal, church and Lamb, Israel and Abba. (This is also a protection against the false perception that the "eunuch lifestyle" is somehow automatically holier than the lifestyle of marriage and family. That's just **not** so.)

So the bridal paradigm is eternally anchored—deep in the Heart of God. The **Heart-womb** of God is Woman. The bridal paradigm is, therefore, pre-creation; it's that old. So when it feels like God's "after you," **remember**—he's hanging out his Heart for you. He's coming to get you 'cause he **likes** you—**just like you are**. He really does. That's why he had "Dr. Bickle" induce love-labor through "Friends of the Bridegroom." It's a paradigm shift to "deliver" us over into Abba, and qualify us for **the** party of all wedding parties.

CHAPTER 20

Israel as God's Wife

——➤•〇•◄——

This one's easy as ABC.

A. God Married Jewel Israel
See Ezekiel 16:6-8

⁶"'Then I passed by, and I said to you, "Live!" ⁷I made you grow like a plant of the field. You grew up and developed and became the **most beautiful of jewels**. ⁸"'Later I passed by, and when I looked at you and saw that you were old enough for love, I spread the corner of my garment over you. **I gave you my solemn oath and entered into a covenant with you, declares the Sovereign LORD, and <u>you became mine.</u>**" This is marriage covenant language, and the rest of the chapter shows this.

B. God Divorced Adulterous Israel
Jeremiah 3:8, "**I gave faithless Israel her**

certificate of divorce and sent her away because of all her adulteries."

Hosea 2:3, "Rebuke your mother, rebuke her, **for she is not my wife, and I am not her husband.** Then she will say, 'I will go back to **my husband as at first,** for then I was better off than now.' **No one will take her out of my hands."** This proves God wants Israel back.

C. **God Wants Israel Back**
(Still Hosea 2)

[14]"Therefore I am now going to **allure her**; I will **lead her** into the desert and **speak tenderly to her**. There **I will give her back** her vineyards, and will make the Valley of Achor a door of hope. **There she will sing** as in the days of her youth, as in the day she came up out of Egypt.

[16]"In that day," declares the LORD, **"you will call me 'my husband';** (She <u>is</u> coming back.)

[19] "I will betroth you to me forever; (**"no one will take her out of my hands."**)

I will betroth you in righteousness and justice, in love and compassion.

[20]"**I will betroth you** in faithfulness, and you will acknowledge the LORD. [23]I will plant her **for myself <u>in the land</u>;** I will show my love to the one I called 'Not my loved one.' I will say to those called 'Not my people, "You are my people'; and they will say, 'You are my God.'"

CHAPTER 21

Israel as God's Bridal Suite

————➤•◦•◀——————

Riding White Horse Bridal Path at the foot of Prophet Mountain, I met three horses head on. Bridal bells jangled from their bridles. Engraved on the first was "Israel Bridal Suite"—on the second, "The Church Inside Israel"—on the third, "Israel-church Oneness with God." As I pondered, I realized (1) The Israel-bridal connection goes back to Abraham. (2) It's an **eternal** covenant connection that guarantees Abraham's family eternal, intimate relations with God. This comes about by God's stepping out to work in nations that are **not** biologically connected with Abraham. From non Abrahamic people, **through** Yeshua, **Israel's** Messiah, Abba will make up a bride (the church) for his Son. This bride will fall in love with Israel; will accept her as her mother and be submerged, or grafted, into oneness with her to form a (re)new(ed) Israel as Abba's wife. (3) God will passionately love the church-infused Israel as his wife, form his one new-humanity nation in her, and reach out to gather in all nations into oneness with him.

God's **national** bridal suite speaks of a place where God comes to know a **nation** intimately until oneness with him is reached.

(**Note break:** Webster defines **intimacy**: "pertains to the essential nature of something"— defines **oneness** as singleness, the quality of being one; unity, the quality of being at one. . . ; wholeness, oneness of personality. Orr ["The International Bible Commentary with the NIV", p710] defines "to know": "The first Bible word for the private relation of husband and wife. . . ." [Gen. 4:1 AV], a word which involves the whole personality, with unveiling and opening on the one hand, appreciation and appropriation on the other.")

God's bridal suite then is the place where God unveils, and opens his essential nature and personality to be appreciated and appropriated. God "knows" the bedroom nation in singleness of being one, unity of being **at** one, and wholeness of oneness of personality. The **nation** then bears God's image, and becomes the heart of God in earth to pump out his passion into the nations.

First horse: Israel Bridal Suite. Yeshua is the Messiah of **Israel**, King of the **Jews**—written on his death stake. He became the blood sacrifice for **Israel's entrance** into Adonai's bedroom as a nation. Messiah took all their national sins on

Himself. As High Priest, he "wore" and bore the **nation** into God's presence. In this sense, Yeshua Messiah "took on" Israel, **embodied** Israel. Those who chose to do so could begin, through him, to make bridal preparations. His body-blood washes out their national sin, along with their personal sins as they accept it. The **Spirit** of Life (life in his resurrected blood) **hovers over the whole nation** to sprinkle it clean and bring it alive—raise it from the dead. Jewish believers in Yeshua Messiah are laying down their lifeblood to "lay the bloodlines" throughout the nation for national resurrection and Bridegroom preparation. The church will give lifeblood transfusions into these bloodlines to resurrect the **nation** of Israel, and, in oneness with her, share Adonai's bridal-key. Therefore, God pours Himself out in glory on his church. He desires his church **unify and focus** on Israel 'til Mount Zion explodes with a burst of bridal passion. **That** will resolve the Middle East crisis and get back for God his Hebrew wife. As Lamb's bride pours all bridal preparation toward Mount Zion, God's Nuptial Bank there receives deposits, builds up a magnetic force field, and pulls Adonai's Bridegroom feet down to strike that spot. (Lightning strikes the ground out of the sky that way.) As promised, he will bring his holy ones, **new** Jerusalem with him to settle down in glory over the old city and (re)create Abba's bedroom. Son's bride and Father's wife love-melt into Oneness, even as Father and Son are one.

Listen also to the dialogue between the Bridegroom and the non Jewish woman with the demonized daughter (Matthew 15:21-28; Mark 7:25-28):

Woman: "Lord, **Son of David**, have mercy on me!"

Jesus: (silence)

Disciples to Jesus: "Lord, send her away; **she keeps crying** after us."

Jesus to all: "I was sent **only** to the lost sheep of **Israel.**"

Woman (kneeling and weeping) to Jesus: "Lord, help me!"

Jesus: "**First,** let the children eat all they want; it's not right to take **the children's bread** and toss it to their dogs."

Woman: "Yes, Lord, but even the dogs under the table eat the **children's** crumbs."

Jesus: "Woman, you have great faith! Your request is granted."

Her daughter was healed right then. Where's **Jesus** focusing? "I was sent **only** to the lost sheep of **Israel**!" The woman's faith found no fault **whatever** with his statement. She lowered herself **way on down** to get Jewish crumbs: "Even the dogs under the table eat **the children's** crumbs." **When she was called a dog, she kept right on coming.** By being under-the-table thankful for Jewish crumbs, she saved her daughter, and felt Yeshua's love woo her, a non Jew, toward God's bridal suite. Think of Jesus as Israel (Jacob), the woman as the church, the girl as Christian converts. More to say, Yeshua? "Yes. **On that day** you will **know** (experience intimately) that **I am in my Father, and you in me, and I in**

you." (See John 14:20 NRSV)

Second horse: The Church Inside Israel. Why not Israel in the church? Why Israel and not the church? Adam and Eve had given away creation. God needed someone in enemy territory to switch sides, but nobody would listen to him. Poor God! One day, a nobody named Abraham said, "Huh? Did I hear somebody? I think I heard **Somebody.**" He did; Abraham and God talked—got to be good friends. God told Abe his problem, and Abe was willing to get involved. Friendship developed into covenant relationship. God said, "Tell you what I'll do, Abe. If you'll receive My presence, I'll put in the Power for this project." Abe said, "I **like** Your company; I'll do it." God promised him, "Stick with me, and I'll make out of your family a great **nation.** You're my friend, Abraham." So Israel is like Abraham to God. I don't want God to break his promise to his friend. I don't want him to break promises to me; I want to know I can **count** on him. Paul said to me (from Romans), "Pelham, you can **count** on God; he didn't reject Israel, as **bad** as they've been. He won't reject you either, as **bad** as you've been. His nature holds a power called grace." "It is no longer by works (not Israel's, not mine, not yours); if it were, grace would no longer be grace." (Romans 11:6)

Nation-wise, why not Israel? I call Paul, the Jew, to the stand. Paul, you're God's first apostle to the non-Jews; what do you have to say on this subject? (See Romans 9:1-8) "I speak the truth in Christ about **the people of Israel.** Theirs **is** the

adoption as sons; theirs **is** the **divine glory**, theirs **is** the **covenants**, theirs **is** the **receiving of the law**, theirs **is** the **temple worship** and **the promises**. Theirs **are the patriarchs**, and from them **is** traced the **human ancestry of Christ, who is God** over all. It is **not** as though God's word had failed. God **has not failed** his friend. For not all who are descended from Israel are Israel. On the contrary, it is through **Isaac** (type of Christ) that Abraham's offspring will be counted. The offspring nation is coming through Yeshua Messiah, but **it is still coming.** In other words, it is not **all** of the natural children who are God's children, but it is the children of the promise through Isaac, fulfilled through Yeshua, who are Abraham's offspring. **They** will form the promised nation." Paul's not finished: (See Romans 2:9-11) "There will be trouble and distress for every human being who does evil: **first** for the Jew, then for the Gentile; but glory, honor and peace for everyone who does good: **first** for the Jew, then for the Gentile. For God does not show favoritism. Who gets judged first? The Jew. Who gets rewarded first? The Jew. So, does God play favorites? **No! God keeps promises!**

    Third horse: Israel-Church Oneness With God. What's God's passion about the church connection with Israel? It is for the church to let him love her **through Yeshua** and use her to get Israel back for Himself and keep his promise to Abraham. This happens as Bridegroom Christ brings his church-bride home to his Abba's house where Adonai Elohim will receive him and his wedding party. That home is Israel. That's where the bridal suite's located—both Father's and Son's. That's where God keeps his promise to Abraham and his friends. Ask Zechariah: "On that day, Adonai's feet will stand **on the Mount of Olives, east of Jerusalem.**" (See Zechariah 14:1, 4.) That's where he lets whoever, of all nations, get in on his family-oneness plan. He'll take anybody who'll get bride-ready. Passion will pick up there when Son gets his bride into Father **in order for Father to get back his Jewish wife, Israel.** Intimate Oneness on a national scale will be **on**! Then the LORD Adonai, my God Elohim, will come, and all the holy ones with him. On that day his feet will stand on the Mount of Olives. On that day, fresh water will flow out from Jerusalem. The LORD Adonai will be king over the whole earth. **Jerusalem will be raised up and remain in its place**. The church is included **there in Jerusalem**— not splintered all over everywhere, doing its **own** thing. Jerusalem will be inhabited; **never again** will it be destroyed. Jerusalem will be **secure**. On that day, great panic. On that day, HOLY TO THE LORD **on the horse's bells.** On that day? Definitely **not** business as usual. Everything is done with passion.

Closing: Bridegroom Yeshua is the resurrected Lamb there on Mount Zion. The church, the "called out ones," follow the Lamb wherever **he** leads, which is **on Mount Zion, not** where they vote to go in the world. These "called out ones" include Jews and Gentiles. The remnant of Yeshua Messiah trusters is pulled from the Jews—the remnant of true

Jesus believers are pulled from the non Jews. They are baptized into One and all made to drink of one Spirit. Today, Yeshua is leading all true listeners into God's Bedroom for the nations—there "on the Mount of Olives, east of Jerusalem," and all over Israel. Passionate increase of Gentile love-labor intensifies the force field. As Abba's love pours into Israel from his church world-wide, that mighty force-field on the Mount of Olives pulls stronger for new Jerusalem to be pulled down over old Jerusalem. Again, why this way? Abraham listened to God when nobody else would. God **promised**— with blood. Church is all about getting Israel back to God as his wife, in order for him to keep his promise and release his love out through Israel to the nations. (See Isaiah 61, 62.) So it's: Judgment—Jew first, Blessing—Jew first, Kingdom—Jew first, Bedroom—Jew first, **in Jerusalem**.

What all will happen in earth? Whatever's required to make it new. Joel speaks about it in chapter two, and Obadiah says six times that Israel on Mount Zion will, by a fire in Jacob and a flame in Joseph, dispossess the ones who dispossessed her, and **"Those who have been saved shall go up to Mount Zion to rule. . . and the kingdom shall be the LORD'S."** From the Lord's kingdom on Mount Zion, Jewel Israel, possessing Yeshua-Abba's heart, with the church inside her, throbs out bridal passion throughout Abba's creation. God's got his dream garden back.

(See Isaiah 66 for the following.)

"[1]This is what the LORD says: [7]'Before she goes

into labor, she gives birth; before the pains come upon her, she delivers a son.' [8]Who has ever heard of such a thing? Who has ever seen such things? Can a country be born in a day or a nation be brought forth in a moment? **Yet no sooner is Zion in labor than she gives birth to her children.**

[9]**Do I bring to the moment of birth and not give delivery?' says the LORD.**

'Do I close up the womb when I bring to delivery?' says your God.

[10]"Rejoice with Jerusalem and be glad for her, all you who love her;

rejoice greatly with her, all you who mourn over her.

[11]"<u>**For you will nurse and be satisfied at her comforting breasts;**</u>

you will drink deeply and delight in her overflowing abundance.' [12]For this is what the LORD says: 'I will extend peace to her like a river, and the wealth of nations like a flooding stream; <u>**you will nurse and be carried**</u> on **her** arm and dandled on **her** knees.

[13]**"As a mother comforts her child, so will I comfort you;** and you will be comforted over Jerusalem.'

[14]"When you see this, your heart will rejoice and you will flourish like grass; the hand of the LORD will be made known to his servants, but his fury will be shown to his foes.

[15]"See, **the LORD is coming with fire**, and his chariots are like a whirlwind; he will bring down his anger with fury, and his rebuke with flames of fire.

¹⁶For with fire and with his sword the LORD will execute judgment upon all men, and many will be those slain by the LORD.

¹⁸"And I, because of their actions and their imaginations, am about to come and **gather all nations** and tongues, and **they will come** and see my glory.

¹⁹"I will set a sign among them, and **I will send some of those who survive to the nations.** They will proclaim my glory among the nations. <u>**20And they will bring all your brothers, from all the nations, to my holy mountain in Jerusalem**</u> as an offering to the LORD.

²²" 'As **the new heavens and the new earth** that I make will endure before me,' declares the LORD, '**so will your name and descendants endure**. ²³From one New Moon to another and from one Sabbath to another, **all mankind will come** and bow down before me,' says the LORD."

CHAPTER 22

Heftzivah:
"My-Delight-Is-In-Her"

——————>>-0-<<——————

"**A**rise, shine [Yerushalayim], for your light has come, the glory of ADONAI has risen over you. For although darkness covers the earth and thick darkness the peoples; on you ADONAI will rise; over you will be seen his glory. **Nations will go toward your light and kings toward your shining splendor. Raise your eyes and look around; they are all assembling and coming to you;** your sons are coming from far off, your daughters being carried on **their nurses'** hips.

"Then you will see and be radiant, your heart will throb and swell with delight; for the riches of the seas will be brought to you, the wealth of nations will come to you. Foreigners will rebuild your walls, their kings will be at your service. Your gates will always be open, they will not be shut by day or by night, so that people can bring you the wealth of nations, with their kings led in procession. For the nation or kingdom that won't serve you will perish; yes, those nations will be utterly destroyed. **I will make you the pride of the ages**, a joy for many generations. You will drink the milk of nations, you will nurse at royal breasts and know that I, ADONAI, am your Savior, that I am the Mighty One of Ya'akov.

"I will make **shalom** your governor and righteousness your taskmaster. **Violence will no longer be heard in your land**, desolation or destruction within your borders; instead, you will call your walls Salvation and your gates Praise. All your people will be **tzaddikim** (priests); they will **inherit the land forever**; they will be the branch I planted, my handiwork, in which I take pride. The smallest will grow to a thousand, **the weakest will become a mighty nation**. I, ADONAI, **when the right time comes**, will quickly bring it about.

"For Tziyon's sake I will not be silent, for Yerushalayim's sake I will not rest, **until her vindication shines out brightly** and her salvation like a blazing torch. **The nations will see your vindication** and all kings your glory. Then you will be called by a new name which ADONAI himself will pronounce. **You will be a glorious crown in the hand of ADONAI, a royal diadem held by your God**. You will not longer be spoken of as Abandoned or your land be spoken of as Desolate; rather, you will be called **'My-Delight-Is-In-Her,'** and your land **'Married.'** For ADONAI delights in you, and **your land will be married**—as a young man marries a young woman, your sons will marry you; as a bridegroom rejoices over the bride, your God will rejoice over you.

I have posted watchmen on your walls, Yerushalayim; they will never fall silent, neither by day nor by night. You who call on ADONAI, give yourselves no rest; and give him no rest **till he restores Yerushalayim** and makes it a praise on earth. Go on through, **go on through the gates**, clear the way for the people! **Build up a highway, build it up!** Clear away the stones! Raise a banner for the peoples! ADONAI has proclaimed to the end of the earth, "Say to the daughter of Tzion, 'Here, your Salvation is coming! Here, his reward is with him, and his recompense is before him.' They will call them The Holy People, The Redeemed of ADONAI. You will be called 'Sought-After,' 'City-No-Longer-Abandoned.'

"For, look! I create new heavens and a new earth; past things will not be remembered, they will no more come to mind. So be glad and rejoice forever in what I am **creating**; for look! I am making Yerushalayim a joy, and her people a delight. I will rejoice **in Yerushalayim** and take joy in my people." (See Isaiah 60-66 CJB)

Isaiah 46 [3] "Listen to me, **O house of Jacob**, all you who remain of the **house of Israel**, you whom **I have upheld since you were conceived**, and have carried since your birth.

[4] Even to your old age and gray hairs, I am he,

I am he who will sustain you. I have made you and I will carry you; **I will sustain you and I will rescue you.**

9   Remember the former things, those of long ago; I am God, and there is no other; I am God, and there is none like me.

10 I make known the end from the beginning, **from ancient times, what is still to come.** I say: My purpose will stand, and **I will do all that I please.**

11 What I have said, **that** will I bring about; what I have planned, **that** will I do.

12 Listen to me, you stubborn-hearted, you who are far from righteousness.

13 I am bringing my righteousness near, it is not far away; and my salvation will not be delayed.

I will grant salvation to **Zion**, (Church, get **into** Zion.) my splendor to **Israel**." (Church, get **into** Israel.)

Church, **quit** trying to **replace** Israel and get **into** Israel—and share his splendor **there**—where he **keeps saying** it will be—in earth, in earth, **in earth!** He made known from ancient times **what is still to come.** "Avraham is Our father in God's sight because he trusted God as the one who gives life to the dead (to dead people, dead marriages, dead church, dead nation of Israel) and **calls nonexistent things into existence.**" (Rom 4:17 CJB)

CHAPTER 23

Please Do—Let Love on Through!

━━━━━●━◄━━━

This chapter is from Pelham and DeDe's Song of Solomon-based marriage contract. Our focus, destiny is to be one of those "third couples" in God's 3-thru of (1) Christ and the Church, (2) Abba and the nation of Israel, (3) humankind husband and wife. We aim to love each other as do Christ and the church, as do God and Israel. We remember this prayer of Jesus: "Father, I desire that those also, whom you have given me, **may be with me where I am** (He's in Father), to see my glory, which you have given me because **you loved me** before the foundation of the world. Righteous Father, the world does not know you, but I know you; and these know that you have sent me. [26]I made your name known to them, and I will make it known, **so that the love with which you have loved me may be in them,**

and I in them." (John 17:24-26 NRSV) From that, I
know I'm destined to have Father love and to love
with Father love—love Jesus with Father love—love
creation with Father love—love all with Father love.
Therefore, through Jesus and his faith living in me,

I identify with Father, look at my wife through
Father eyes (as being not only my wife but his wife),
pull in **Father love** out of the heavens, love **my wife**
with Father-Son love, then we as one, impart Father-
Son love out to others **in earth now.**

Hope this makes a landing in your understanding. We don't aim to embarrass you in our show of
love today for God and each other. We're baring and
sharing our hearts, trusting God to bring us all closer
to him. We invite you to be sensitive to love today, to
"give in" to it. How much of the world lies unloved
because those claiming God are **ashamed** to show
love? Don't **let** shame make you send love off to
hide. People today are **desperate** for it.

God gave us a marriage manual in the Bible so
we could know how to let love live in our marriages.
Humankind has been cheated out of this for generations. Should not man and woman be encouraged
and empowered to lay hold of God's provision for
our lives and relationships? Would this not include
bringing sexual passion in off the streets and back
into God? Why not **learn** how to love and give a
generation a little more than "Kill those hormones
now! They'll get you in trouble!" **No! God** put those
hormones there! The serpent **stole** passion from God
and sold it on the streets. It's time to take it back to
God in the Garden of Eden. This marriage manual is

called the "Song of Solomon." Today, we are using the faith of Jesus given us to plug into these characters of "The Beloved" (groom) and "The Shulamite" (bride) in this Jewish Song, trusting God for **this "S-O-S" relationship** in our marriage **here now in earth.** Then, a few months down the road, we won't be sending out "S-O-S" disaster calls. There are forces out to do us all in by cramming us down in the war bin. Let's rise in faith into his love for an indisputable and indestructible imprint in Jesus' name.

Of course, the next few minutes will be different. What did you come way out here in the fields to see? More tradition? Why did you come out here? To experience "same-o-same-o-stuff?" You didn't have to drive hours for **that**. So, reach with us as we hold out our hearts to catch a fresh love breeze blowing out of heaven. How 'bout it?

God Is Love

What is love (God) all about? Marriage—true marriage. He's about caring family—about a safe haven home. He's about children—caressed, cherished, cuddled and kept. He's about children being constrained, controlled and compelled—counseled, compassionate, and complete. His love is about **children who conquer**—in pure love, giving from God, cradle to **"save,"** 'til these compassionate, caring children **conquer the grave.** This love hugs a cross so it won't have to hug a dead child.

We're talking about love that **abhors** evil and men's wars hard enough to wage God's war, battling

181

one with the Prince of Peace, **to end all wars**. This love is **passionately jealous**—hot enough to decimate, obliterate, incinerate and annihilate all competition—every pocket of prejudice—every hidden, hideous, hard-hearted, hate hut of violence from here to hell—**to make way for love to flourish and bloom unbruised in a new earth.**

Religion, war, hatred and violence? God! Strike with your jealous **love-fire** the whole **hell** of it—dilute and dissipate the very **smell** of it! Demolish, destroy and devastate the dilapidated **shell** of it. Let its traps be tripped, trampled and trodden. Let its tyranny be toppled—**totally**, and let its prisoners **go free! But for this to happen, we gotta let!** Let the people go free to love free! Let the children go free to **be** loved, to **learn to love** free! **Let! Let! Come On! Let's let love!**

Let the love birds nest and sing as they please—Let the baby cradles swing in the breeze

Let love rule till love reigns—Let love be loved without any shame

Let a man and a woman love God-children into creation

Let man and wife begin a love nation, perpetuate love regeneration

Let man and wife **experience** love's full revelation, be held by heaven's sensation

Let couples reestablish love's reputation, build God's new humanity nation

Let, let, let! Come on, let's let!

Let heaven keep coming on down—'Til heaven walks **all over** the ground

Let heaven's harps make their sound—Let all that hidden manna be found

Let love come on down—Move on out, overflow and abound!

Let, let, let! Come on, let's let!

Jesus died "damned" for love to live free—So it could spill out into you and me

Tragedies explode today at the drop of a hat—**Still** mankind fights—blind as a bat

Let love through, please! **Let's get the drift!** Before God wipes us out in the graveyard shift!

God! We know you're **not** dead so soften our head—We yield our heart, to eat your sweet bread

Now where, in this hell on earth, do we choose to be? **Will** we stand up for love to go free?

Not just church-front lukewarm stuff, no luster a-tall—Real **passion** 'til the hot tears fall

Love the Lord your God with all you be—All you are, have got, and ever will see

Love any of humankind that's in true need—With the same love you'd hope to receive.

Jesus, you proved, sagging on a piece o' tree—Just how far you'd stretch your love to me

So with all I am, have, and ever shall be—I **will** stand up, shake off shackles and let love free!"

Welcome, my friends, to love—and war! Love that's hung up in a peace-fighting war

In order to **end** all wars so that love can—Rise up to rule in the son of man.

Here's the Solomon's Song, Southern Style, that I wrote and sang at the wedding. After I sang, I got my answer in the **most beautiful** Shulamite love-song-dance **Missouri** ever witnessed!

DeDe Girl

DeDe girl, you're my Shugah – Sweetened on the living Vine

A soft love grape full of heaven's honey – Turning my water into wine

You're turning my water into wine

DeDe girl , you're my Shugah – I want you to be all mine

I'll fill you with love on Fire – And burn your water into wine

I'll burn your water into wine

DeDe girl , you're my Shugah – Ride with me on the Wind

The white horse loping out of heaven – Into places love's never been.

Riding into places love's never been

DeDe girl, you're my Shugah – Riding the holy Wind free

Catching Father's love burning us one – Shugah, will you marry me?

Shugah, will you marry me?

DeDe girl, you're my Shugah – I'm handing-to-you my heart's key

Will you give it a turn and come on in? Shugah, will you marry me?

Shugah, will you marry me?

DeDe girl, you're my Shugah – Jesus living in you set free

God making us one in Spirit-Love – Will you marry the Jesus in me?

DeDe girl, will you marry me?

DeDe girl, you're my Shugah – Tell me, Shugah, can you see

Enough Jesus in me to keep you loved? See enough to say yes to me?

DeDe girl, will you marry me? Dede girl, will you marry me?

Oh! If only you could have heard her and **seen** her dance, you would have **known** she danced a great big **yes!** What Shugah? You want to say something? Okay—have at it. Wait—is it mushy? Long live Love—and pass the "mush!"

CHAPTER 24

This is Woman!

⟹•◦•⟸

"The man said, 'This is now bone of my bones and flesh of my flesh; she shall be called 'woman,' for she was taken out of man.' For this reason a man will leave his father and mother and be united to his wife, and they will become one flesh." (Genesis 2:23, 24) Today, Adam could say,

"Woman! I **like** this **creature**!" Growing up, I heard this song: "Women, women, women! What you gonna do about 'em? You can't live with 'em and you can't live without 'em?" I think men **still** wonder—what to "do about 'em." But did you ever stop to think—just stop! For one minute. Imagine a **whole** planet—nothing but **men!** See what I'm saying? I'm **out of here**! You can have it. Well, Adam didn't have a planet full of men. He just had a garden full of creation, I reckon, and no woman— 'til God said, "Close your eyes; no fair peeking." Then, "How do you like **this**?" Adam: "I **like** this woman!"

Men, see if this will help us know what to "do about 'em."

She's to be prized—not "propertied." This is woman—God's style.

She's to be borne—not bundled, beaten, bruised and battered. This is true woman.

She's to be re-ceived, not de-ceived—touched, not trampled. This is woman.

She's to be loved tenderly, not lashed merci-lessly—bosomed, not bashed. This is woman.

She's to be treasured, not trashed—manned, not mashed. This is woman.

She's to be honored, not garnered—cared for, not cursed at. This is woman.

She's to be liberated, not castigated—sent, not rent. This is woman.

She's to be used, not ab-used—caressed, not harassed nor harnessed. This is woman.

She's to be protected, not subjected. Uh-oh! Did I write that? Couldn't the tons of energy men spend trying to subject women (under the mask of "submission") be better spent bringing **ourselves** into submission to God? Wouldn't all our **macho** manliness stuff be more fruitful if directed into making **us men** submitted to God? Generally speaking, a woman has little trouble **submitting** to a man who's sold out to God. Let's go on.

Woman is to be pro-jected, not re-jected—kissed sweetly, not hissed scornfully.

She's to be provided for, not punished—privil-edged, not just hedged and edged.

She's to be led into, not driven out of—pointed upward, not pressed downward.

She's to be a-ligned, not ma-ligned—delivered, not destroyed. This is woman.

She's to be called out, not squalled at—fired up, not fired at. This is woman.

She's to be helped, not hammered —held, not hurt. This is woman.

She's to be found, not fixed—loosed, not bound. This is woman.

She's to be tendered, not rendered—oiled, not spoiled. This is woman.

She's to be labored with, not lunged at—cradled, not crippled. This is woman.

She's to be equipped, not stripped—empowered, not embroiled. This is woman.

She's to be stroked, not choked—cloaked, not provoked. This is woman.

This is **woman** and we could go on and on about God's crowning creation, but there is a tricky part. She's to be postured but not pedestalled—con-verted but not per-verted. This too is woman.

She's to be worshipped **with**, not worshipped—not her femininity, not her foxy, not her finery, fash-ion, **form or figure**. She is **not** to be worshipped! Her shallow nature (from old Adam) is what fuels a desire inside her to be lifted to an **icon pedestal.** She's a creature of God, who herself needs to worship God. She belongs **to him**. Her deepest inner self longs for God and be-longs to God. Her deepest longings are for deliverance from her shallow self up into God. This too is woman, but, like first Adam, and **like God, "I like this creature,"** says **Last** Adam, then adds, "Work with Me to get her in her true destiny and keep her there. I'll reward you richly."

Part Five:
Father Mothers
Creation Through Israel

CHAPTER 25

A New Wineskin Stretcher for Mount Zion New Wine

She's a-coming all-'round the mountain, when she
    comes (Repeat)
She's a-coming all-'round the mountain, to brood all
    over Zion
She's a-coming all-around the mountain when she
    comes

If you don't have the **big** picture, you don't
know where the **little** one fits in. If any of this
messes with your theology—ah-h-h, **far** be it from
me—but if it **does**, feel free to change it! Anyway,
saying like I see. Theology they fed me five decades
didn't do me right. Hope your "feeders" did better.
This is **really** a big picture. Take little bites, don't

stuff your mouth, and **chew your food.** (Yep, I got kids—and "grands." One reason I'm writing this!) Be blessed.

♦ God created one man—only one man. He "formed" Eve from this one man. There's no mention that God breathed (separately from Adam) into her the breath of life for her to become a **separate** living soul.

♦ This man disobeyed. God came looking for Adam—not Eve, not "them". Adam had to be put out of the garden to keep him from eating the wrong stuff and living forever, messed up with God. Eve got thrown out with him.

♦ Move on down the road. God came a-calling and Abraham answered.

♦ This resulted in a "mankind" coming forth, chosen of God, to be brought back into right relationship with him, to be used by him to offer good-standing to his entire creation that was living in its messed up condition.

♦ This mankind ended up being called Israel, or the Jews. They didn't stick to the plan any better than did Adam One.

♦ Last Adam Yeshua had to come bail out Adam-One-Israelites, Jews, all creation.

♦ In the process, Last Adam had the gall to mess with Adam One's messed up Jewish religion.

♦ You know the scene, if not the whole routine.

♦ Last Adam fooled 'em—stepped **outta the grave** blowing and going, romping and stomping!

♦ Even while Adam One Jews were becoming Last Adam Jews, God had Paul waiting in the wings with a back up plan, **just in case.** Sure enough, the Last Adam Jews didn't make it to home plate without getting tagged out. Wouldn't you just know it!

♦ Gentiles ended up with the good news and Paul brought forth churches "among the nations." He laid it out to the non-Jews, "Reach back and get the Jews. God wants one new humanity. Jews and Gentiles must become one new man because God started out with one man, and he's got eternity to get it back like he wants it—one man."

♦ God worked hard at it in Martin Luther's generation—didn't happen. Sorry, God; all our fault—again.

♦ Travel on down the trail; God wanted his people to be the head and not the tail!

♦ God tried to bail it out through Apostle J. W. Pruett, Senior in the 1970's. Made good headway till 1976. Laid a foundation. The chosen got frozen in forms, danced to Jezebel demons and dawdled away their destiny, leaving Pruett's foundation like a bare concrete slab.

♦ 1994. God hit Toronto: Toronto Blessing.

♦ 1995. God hit Pensacola: Fuel on the fire.

♦ 1996. God struck Smithton, Missouri—middle of **nowhere**—called "The Cornfield Revival." God hammered away at the Gentiles, "Don't miss out like the nation of Israel did first time around by holding on to their old corrupted national religious rituals. Get **real** with God." While God was talking like that to non Jews, he was pleading with Jews, "Don't be blinded like your early ancestors (and like the Gentiles for 2,000 years), and end up failing to host me in the middle of a new earth—get on **my** plan. I want one new man, one new humanity, all living in love together in a garden setting. Be smart enough to know that if I want it, I **will** have it 'fore it's over—one way or the other. **Cooperate** with me here."

♦ 1998. "Bethlehem Stable" opened as part of Shiloh Estates. God tapped some more little guys—zapped a little prayer group. International House of Prayer (IHOP) opened, and in a few months, prayer, praise, and worship was going up to God 24/7—"going 'til Jesus comes," says Mike Bickle. "Friends of the Bridegroom" (FOTB) ministry was born. A **"Mandate for Israel"** ministry was announced. **Focus** started swinging toward Israel. God miraculously provided 1.1 million dollars in an IHOP offering and **all of it went to Bibles for Soviet Jews.** Forerunner Christian Fellowship was formed with one of the twenty congregations being charged to launch the Israel Mandate. Finally, God had somebody's attention going in his direction—Israel's direction.

♦ God's one new man will, of course, have to be of one flesh, just like Adam was of one flesh, like Adam and Eve were to be one flesh—just like husbands and wives were to be one flesh and perpetuate one flesh—one family flesh—**of God.**

♦ God is Spirit. Jesus is God. Jesus is Spirit and Truth. Those who get into his presence must do it by Spirit and Truth.

♦ Therefore, to God, spirit is far more "real" than the natural and physical. The One who is Spirit created all that's "natural" and "physical."

♦ When God looked at Adam and Eve, he saw them as one, even though, after Eve was brought forth from within Adam, they appeared physically as two. God saw them as one because they were created as one humanity. After the creation of all the other stuff, Adam was first formed from the dust, then Eve was brought forth from **that** formation and **formed** (with physical-alongside-capability) from Adam's insides.

♦ In God's plan, obedience of Adam (and Eve) was to mature a full flowing between the two so Eve's spirit could flow inside Adam's spirit, and she could still move **physically** outside of Adam and flow **spiritually**—still one with Adam—separate, but not independent. God saw them as one before and after the moment he brought Eve forth from inside Adam and set the separate-but-not-independent flowing in motion. To God it is the **flowing** that's **primary**—the one flowing—because, what is the flowing? The flowing is spirit. This flowing between the two formations of flesh joins the two bodies of flesh and makes the flesh one flesh. Since God is Spirit, the flowing of spirit through both bodies of flesh makes and keeps them one flesh—**so far as God's concerned.** That's how **he** sees them. His eyes see **deeper**.

♦ Jesus, while appearing in the upper room after his resurrection, said that a spirit does not have flesh and bone like he has. He said nothing

197

about his blood.
- In Leviticus God says the life is in the blood.
- The cleansing work of the blood is now done by the blood of Jesus which became the Spirit of Life in the Holy of Holies.
- If Jesus' glorified body has flesh, bone and blood-become-Spirit (in place of blood), then flesh is quickened by the Spirit and the flowing of the Spirit is throughout the flesh or the body and sustains it.
- This being the case, the flowing that was present in the garden was restored with Jesus taking his blood into the Holy of Holies and becoming a Life-giving Spirit—but still a Spirit capable of flesh being clothed upon it and capable of entering flesh and possessing flesh and occupying flesh as living quarters.
- With the flowing restored through the Son, then Father looks and begins to see one flowing beginning again because the flowing is what? The flowing is Spirit. The flowing is his Son. "The Lord is that Spirit". (2 Cor 3:17, "Now the Lord is the Spirit; and where the Spirit of the Lord is, there is liberty.") He joins a man and wife with this restored flowing and in that flowing they are one flesh.
- Whatever is joined into this flowing becomes one flesh. As children are born in this flowing, they are born into this one network of flesh.
- As we are all baptized into Holy Spirit, and this Spirit flows through all, we are all immersed or submerged into this network and this one flesh

in God.

♦ As Jesus takes headship of this network of Spirit flowing, which has become like our arteries and veins that carry our blood of life throughout our physical bodies—as he is given charge of this network, his church, his body, as the firstborn among many brethren, and we become bone of his bone and flesh of his flesh, then that quickening Spirit can cleanse our blood and begin to flow through our blood—as it did his blood—while we're still walking around here looking pretty (spiritually, that is). This flowing begins to change us into that new humanity with the likeness and image of God with which humankind started out.

♦ And, even though we are all physically individual, we are not independent. We are inter-dependent and members one of another in his network. Staying in this one flowing makes us all one flesh from the Father's vantage point and in the Father's eyes (which is the only vantage point that counts for very much eternity).

♦ Therefore, as we walk in obedience, keeping our side of the covenant, when Father looks upon us with his Son's spiritual flesh holding us together, he sees his Son first because his Son is Spirit, one with him. He lives in us and he is what is quickening our mortal bodies. Before Father looks at any part or member of this one flesh, Spirit has so filled his eyes with love for his Son that his love goes ahead of his eyes. Before his eyes fall upon us, Spirit cleanses us from all unrighteousness so that when his eyes do fall on us, his love has already burned out what's not of love, and his love has filled up the holes. Result: all Father sees is Jesus—and us a part of the overall body of his Son.

♦ The Spirit spreads or stretches out through the entire body as arteries, blood vessels—"carriers" throughout the physical body, cleansing and tying formations of flesh together into one body of flesh, pleasing to him and sustaining it through the one flowing from the Son, resting now one in Father. And what part of our Father would you figure all this is flowing out from? Where is your life pumped out from? He is the Source of all life. He is Father, Mother, Son; he is One.

♦ The scripture is fulfilled, "At that day you will know that I *am* in My Father, and you in Me, and I in you." (John 14:20 NRSV) That sounds like we're all one in him—one new humanity.

♦ The one flesh in heaven clothes down upon and begins to transform the one flesh in earth into "new" flesh, becomes one with the one flesh in earth, swallowing up and processing, through Jesus-regeneration, the earth-flesh into oneness with the new heaven flesh, creating a "new earth."

♦ Son was swallowed up into Father. Spirit (called "bride," "wife," "new Jerusalem," "Heart of God," "Womb of the morning") is hovering over Israel and creation. He has "bowed the heavens and come down." Just like he "bowed" over physical creation, over the virgin, Mary, and bows over whoever calls on him, **trusting** in his Name. He's after a bride for his Son who'll help him get his wife, Israel, back. From there, from Zion, God aims to rule it all through his new humanity—Israel based—capitol city, old Jerusalem, made one with new Jerusalem.

♦ Through Son, the earthly bride matures on into Father where males become one with Father to reveal Father in earth. Females become one with the Mother working of God, who is already one with Father, that the Mother side of God may be seen in earth.

♦ Father God, living in new-humanity-males in the new earth and "Mother-God," living in new-humanity-females in the new earth, give birth in the new earth to many brothers (and sisters) of Jesus, the Messiah Son. These children come forth from the womb filled with the Holy Spirit, speaking **new** earth language—tongues of new heaven and new earth, now one language. **God rules!**

♦ Jesus got his bride. Jesus and his wife got Abba's wife, Israel, back. Why, it's just like my brother Hosea heard, saw, and said! (See Hosea 2:14-23)

♦ One family again. One flesh. The Lord our God is one God—now one with his people. Heaven and earth one—no more dividing sea.

♦ Hallelujah and amen. So has it been poured out. So has it been revealed. So has it been spoken. So has it been written anew, my brother John, with Jesus' kind of love, and so I say with you,

♦ **It is finished, and it is done—hallelujah to the reigning Son. It has forever more been done.** If it doesn't look like this out your window right now, put on your **new** specks—and **see it anyhow**—so it <u>can</u> **keep on coming!**

She's a-coming all-'round the mountain, when she
    comes (Repeat)
She's a-coming all-'round the mountain, to brood all
    over Zion
She's a-coming all-'round the mountain when she
    comes

CHAPTER 26

Nation Regeneration

"All Israel will be saved." (See Romans 9-11, esp. 11:26) Five little words. How many lifelong theologians, daily professionals, and Sunday morning quarterbacks have said a say on **those**, do you suppose? This is not to salt or pepper the sages of old. We can offer only what we have. We can share only what we see. What we see and say varies with experiences, revelations, and maturity—not to mention the weightier matters of heart motivations and religious ambitions.

As stated in "Arrested In Shalom Emporium", a **BAM!** thunderbolt struck my own Israel-related theology. You ever had a "where **ever** have I been all this time experience?" Hopefully no, but probably so—if you've lived very long outside your cultural, baby-comfort crib. It's been a few months since my theology went into rearrangement mode about the place of the **literal, geographical, dirt-down-nation** of Israel. That is, as opposed to my longtime, **supposedly,** super spiritual "Israel," made up some- how of a church conglomerate, swinging and swameying in a Christian-like climate somewhere off in space someplace, above the actual dirt-ground of planet earth—maybe in midair suspension, or linger- ing in limbo. I could never really quite get it to come together in my good-sense side. Mind you, not that I didn't work at it seriously for half a century. Now some thoughts to date—backing up a bit here to get a running start.

Here's God—With Our Problem:

He is love. He not only **wants** to love all humankind, he **does it.** We're part of his original idea. Pure love is passionate. God is pure love. He is passionate. Passion is fire. Our God is a consuming Fire—because he is pure passion. God cannot change who he is. He just is—and he is that—consuming, passionate love Fire. Humankind, created by consuming Fire, is given power of choice—yes or no. Do we want the presence of the Fire? Do we not want the Fire? Do we want God? Do we **not** want God? Do we want his Presence? Do we want him living among us? Or even inside us? He can't change who he is. If he comes, he comes **like** he is—**who** he is. He comes loving and he comes burning—and he comes consuming. He cannot shut off his nature that is forever consuming love Passion. When he shows up, he comes consuming.

Anybody want him to show? Anybody yearning for love burning? If not, God is **forced** to keep his distance in order to honor our choice. To come near to love us on up into his heart without our yearning consent would require him to go into override, and he doesn't like to do that. He respects our decision not to be consumed into his love, and just lets us do whatever else we're about doing—at least for a while. Mind you, in that choice, he is **not** covenant-bound to protect, provide, nurture and grow us up in him because **we** have not chosen **his** consuming love. You still with me? He consumes with fiery passionate love. Who wants him? "Wel-l-l-l-l, if he'll just…" Nope. 'Fraid not. He's not a shopping mall where one goes to pick stuff off the shelves as one goes about his own pre-chosen way. There may be a god who works that way, but it is not the God. We're talking about The one God, the Papa of the last David. He comes to swallow up—to consume with burning, love passion. Ultimately, we face this Ultimate Lover—to go one way or another—forever—based on our choice. In our choosing days, do we choose to be consumed into his love? If not, we have most certainly chosen against his love. The former is con-struction, the latter de-struction. We are destined to be structured—either into his love rule, or else ruled out of his love. Am I right about this?

Here's "Hairy" Times:

How close are we to being consumed at the parting of the Way—when we'll be locked into one way forever, either into being constructed into his power of love, or into being "destructed," forever separated from his love? How far is the planet from this climax? How far the people? How far the person? Sobering questions to me. Who knows—except this ultimate consumer lover Himself?

Some think this is why John The Revelator, apostle of love, was weeping in The Revelation (chapter 5). He saw a scroll full of writing on both sides. My guess is that he connected with the old prophet's vision and understood this to be double trouble judgment headed for earth. The time was "hairy" to John for his generation. He wanted to find some way to stay the judgment, but the scroll was **completely** ("seven" is complete) sealed—locked tight. So John was doing **some kind** of crying—weeping, weeping, weeping for God's creation.

John, who wrote all about love, would know the depth of God's love passion available to those who yearned it and chose it. He would also be terrified in knowing that the same intensity of jealous judgment passion would be released **against** all those who spurned the love. The intensity of passion would be the same in either direction—for construction into oneness with love, or for destruction away from love. The love intensity that burns to consume **into** love also burns with the same intensity to consume back **away** from love all those who reject love. So all are **burning**—one way or the other—yearners **and** the spurners—all get the same degree of passion. Yearners turn into love-burners, one with the Love-Burner-God; spurners are burned **away** from, separated back from, the love-burners after they've spurned their final "no" to love.

In other words, rebels against true love and true

peace will be destroyed rather than let them destroy love and peace. Love-Shalom must, and will, burn brightly. "That has already been written, settled," so says the ultimate Lover. In the end, love will win. In the end, will **I** be swallowed up in love—in and one with the ultimate Lover? That's the question.

Here's Today's Deal:

"It was by a revelation that this secret plan was made known to me. I have already written about it briefly, and if you read what I have written, you will grasp how I understand this secret plan concerning the Messiah." Ephesians 3:3-4 (CJB). I'm taking it that "this secret plan concerning the Messiah" **includes** that part of it as revealed in Romans 9-11. The part of this plan involving Israel as a nation came to me by a revelation experience as written in "Arrested In Shalom Emporium."

This ultimate Lover God of creation is not "out for blood" in the bad sense of the saying, at least not today. He's **given** blood; he gave at the office, the one in Israel. He gave:

- ♦ beard snatched, face-caked blood
- ♦ thorn pierced, hair-soaked blood
- ♦ whip-cut, splashed blood,
- ♦ spiked-hands splattered blood
- ♦ feet nail-driven, oozing flood,
- ♦ spear-slashed, gut-spurting blood.

Has God given blood—or has God **not** given blood? And where did Messiah give it? He gave at the office—**in Israel**. The Ancient of Days, our Creator Father God was a full "Donor-Participant" in the bleeding—**in Israel**. So, how long do you figure it'll be before this love donation is blanked from heaven's memory bank? But, blessed be his Name, God is not "out to get blood" judgment for the blood given—not today. I'm **not** saying how long this will hold true after I finish this sentence.

Not out hunting blood today, but God is **out** today. He is out and about—taking care of business—**back at the office where he gave blood**—his office **in Israel.** God has **not** forgotten his people, his promise. He's on a roll, but he's not out to get blood. Who thinks the "Middle East War" going on now is just another of those foreign wars that we cluck our tongues at? And say, "Yeah, too bad about the violence, the bloodshed, and all the suffering, but they're always fighting over something. That whole side of the world is messed up; they killed Jesus, you know. Too bad. We'll say a prayer for them once in a while as we go about our church business as usual. Bless 'em, God, **if it be your will at this time.**"

Here's You (If You Were God):

Let's look a **little** beyond this—at **least** a little. What if you were God? And you gave blood? You gave your child's blood? You gave **all** of your child's blood? (Mothers? I'm asking you too.) What if you were God and you gave all of your child's blood—at the office—**in Israel?** Would the blood running in the streets there now mean any more to you? When you had given all of your own child's blood to **stop violence and bloodshed and usher in a whole era of love and peace?** I have children; I asked myself that question.

Here's God After Something:

The God who's out and about, the God who gave blood—and **made** blood in the beginning—is not out for blood today but he's out for something. He's out for **dirt—blood dirt.** God has already roared out of the heavens, coming after dirt. He hears blood crying out from the dirt. He still hears Abel's blood crying out from the dirt. When God first heard Abel's blood crying—wouldn't surprise me if he set up a sea of blood **right then**—an invisible sea of blood in the earth—**to which he's been adding innocent, obedient blood ever since.** Wouldn't shock me to learn that, right about now, it's up to the horse's bits like John saw in The Revelation. Wouldn't mess up my theology to learn Messiah's love-blood-passion **set the sea on fire.**

Of this one thing I am persuaded since being arrested in the Shalom Emporium, God's after the **very dirt** of Israel that caught the blood of his Son—and sons, and daughters, and children—the **very dirt** that continues to be stained and soaked. "God's not in the real estate business," has someone said? Pray for 'em. They repeated what **Satan** said to them.

Think this way: what if you once had a Garden of love on some real estate with a peaceful plan to spread love throughout your creation, and someone tricked your kids and stole it? Then, one of your children bought it back, but he died doing it. You watched and felt the pain with each drop of blood that drained away his life. You watched blood fall in the courtroom when he stood there to face trumped-up charges. You were looking at the trail of blood as they dragged him down the steps of the courthouse and on down the road. You saw blood still dripping while he clawed his way up a rocky hill. You cried when they spiked and staked him—and the blood soaked the wood. You watched, you agonized as the dirt drank your own flesh-and-blood's blood. And **now** you're telling me you don't care about that dirt? That it means **nothing** to you?

I'd be numb-struck with, "My child loved me to **death** for this dirt. His blood is **forever** in this dirt. I want **this** dirt, not just **some** dirt, **some** where—I want **this blood-dirt.**" And, you know what? If I had the power, I would have the dirt. I would **own** that piece of real estate—every particle of stone, every grain of sand, every bit of grit, every skirt of dirt connected. "**This** real estate caught my child's love-blood, and **it's mine if I live!**"

God has the power. He's definitely after the dirt. That's how I think since being arrested by a Jew— for **the** Jew and for Jews. Okay, just hang on and read on, will you? Hear me out; all I ask. Maybe think some different thoughts while God's **not** out for blood? I set out to restudy for my own under-standing a few scriptures about Israel's God-set destiny with no plan for a theological study. I was after a narrow focus on Scripture directly related to God's dealings, promises, covenants, and plans for the nation of Israel. I had **too many**—deleted **six** pages that seemed less direct than the others, and still printed out **twenty seven** pages (in normal print size). Surprised? I was; it's there—**everywhere**. Been there all this time. Where have **I** been? I'm talking about me. How I could have been so stupid? I was **blinded**, that's how—and I don't want **you** to be blinded. Thank you, Paul, for warning us **not to be caught** on one of those wild olive tree branches that arrogantly set themselves apart from the cultivated, natural-olive-tree Jews who bore us. Such arrogance has certainly stuck us with a messy mass of confused ignorance that God is now torching.

I'm seeing now that **consuming God-Love will swallow up the real estate of Israel**, and, on that very dirt that God lost to the enemy, God will glorify his suffering servant Son-Messiah of Israel in magnificent splendor that will sparkle the planet and dazzle the heavenlies. After all, this Messiah used his own blood to cut the new covenant that was **promised to Israel.** On that day, Israel **got** her Messiah King, the Root and Offspring of David, the King of the **Jews**. He was that day advertised as "The King of the Jews." He is today King of the Jews, Messiah of Israel, the David promised the nation of Israel, the last Adam-Man through whom all humankind may choose to enter into the most holy Presence of the Lover God by yearning for, and yielding into, his all consuming passion.

Here's What I See:

It's about sundown. A Sabbath of "suddenlies" is slipping in close enough to smell. God misses his garden a lot. He needs dirt for his garden. He **likes** the dirt he first picked out—the dirt first Adam gave away that is now blood-dirt. He's paid good blood for it and now he's coming with burning fury after what he paid for—after the **dirt**.

Just so we don't get "replacement-ized" here, and subsequently spiritualized, galvanized and paralyzed to truth reality, I'm talking about the **nation** of Israel. It makes sense to me that God's after his first garden spot of Eden where he can love his wife without distractions—where love can bud and blossom. Here in this love garden his family can, through the suffering-servant Messiah, grow into the servant nation they were destined to be from the beginning. Through this suffering-servant Messiah, this suffering-servant **nation** of Israel can be the Heart of Abba, from which Love-Life flows throughout his creation. "Little Jacob (Israel)" swallowed up in "Big Jacob (Messiah)" puts David's offspring on the throne forever. The little Gideon nation yields to be consumed into the full passion of Yeshua-Abba. Israel is overshadowed by new Jerusalem from above, and the blood-dirt city of Jerusalem is opened to all nations.

The old prophets, including Jeremiah, Isaiah, Ezekiel, Zechariah, Micah, Paul, John, and the others delivered a steady drumbeat message from the God of Abraham, Isaac, and Israel. It went something like this: "Israel, you're really messed up. Israel! You're missing it! Listen and **obey** God. You're in big-time trouble!" Generation to generation, the drumbeat never changed. Most of us may have gotten **that** part—but **missed the kicker**. Even while God was "skinning them alive" through the prophets, God—too many times to ignore—**promises** to "**restore** their 'hide'" as a nation. He absolutely promises this. If you were led by the blind, as was I, **check this out for yourself—please.** Is that asking too much?

God says over and over, "**Whatever** condition the nation of Israel is in, Israel is **mine! Don't** mess around with my wife! Yeah, she's messed up, but she's **my** mess up, **not** yours, so don't you mess around with her. I'll take care of what needs taking care of—**period.** I aim to **fix up** the **mess up** and **she will 'fess up** 'fore this is all **wrapped up.** Don't you **dare** decide to pick and choose just how and what I should do with the Jews!"

Here's Trouble:

A 100 years or so after God mercifully included non Jews into his developing family, a few of these "nons" held one of the first in a long line of church councils. They drew a conclusion and set it forth as a "Church Creed." God's never had time for the brilliancy of their intellectual conclusions: "We've got Jesus. We need **nothing** Hebrew—**nothing!** Who needs Jews? Who cares about Jewish roots? Jews got together against Jesus, didn't they?" And while they, themselves, were writing this up, what were **they** themselves caught up in? Getting together against Jesus! How ironical. Jews also wrote the Bible and were martyred in order to give **them** the gospel.

History is beginning to expose these "great council conclusions" as based on prejudice. They head-hammered out this church creed that became the standard for a "Christian" movement that would veer, at first undetectably, **away and apart** from anything, anyone Jewish. Of course, they used the Bible to back up what they themselves had already hatched up. They said they were Spirit led and this was God. Was it?

I never realized that the "Christian Crusades," in which so many people were slaughtered was, at its heart, directed against the Jews. Did you know that? I was ignorant. You know about the Holocaust. Right? The Holocaust in which 6-12 million Jews and some 8 million others were hanged, butchered, shot, gassed, buried alive, and cooked alive in ovens, many of them babies and children? Did you ever see any of those pictures? Did you know that Hitler said he was only following through on what the "Christians" had set out to do in their crusades and failed to finish? In other words, he was doing what Christians started and didn't have the guts to complete. Did you know Hitler called himself a "Christian"—that he was never excommunicated from the Roman Catholic Church? Did you know that while these people were being led to the ovens there were "Christian" entertainers joyfully singing "Christian" songs, rejoicing that "Christianity" was being "purged of the Jews" and "purified for God." Can you imagine? And Stalin did even worse. I didn't know that either. That's how far behind I've been—but I'm catching on, and I'm catching up.

This is why "Christians" begin the 21st century with such a monstrous mess on our hands:

"Christian" junkyards of divisive denominational-ism, independent empires of hot air charades, crusades, and parades—totally useless to God in his plan to usher in the fullness of his kingdom—**counter**-productive, set against God who has Israel in his heart. What a cruel and crushing "Christian" conglomeration I find myself caught in. Not the people, the **prison** of religion gone creepy crazy!

The old covenant was cut with Abraham, Isaac, and Jacob—all counted as "Jews" since "Jews" is the term used to include their descendents through Isaac. We, as non-Jews, were let in on it, but the covenant was with Jews. The new covenant was cut with Israel, the Jews; we, wild olive tree non-Jews, were graciously given opportunity to be grafted into the natural (Jewish) olive tree. Are we grafted in? Really grafted in?

If we're **really** grafted into the natural Jewish olive tree, won't we have some care about the tree we're grafted into? How can we be grafted in if we care zero about Israel and Jews? And if we don't care about Israel and Jews through whom God reached out to us, what god do we have? Do we have the God of Abraham, Isaac, and Israel who sent Yeshua to be the Messiah of Israel? Do we have the Jesus who died under the tag, "King of the Jews?" Or, have we been duped into following one of those other "lords" that Paul warns us about? If our Jesus is not the one coming down the line from Abraham through the Jews, what is his origin? What "lord" do we have? Have we "minded-up" one in our bril-liancy? To suit our own fancy? Further our own "views," as did our church "fathers?"

Could it be that miracles and healings are so scarce because we've been sold a soapbox savior? Could that be why we're barrel-headed and marble-hearted? "Head too big: heart too little," as Heidi Baker keeps faithfully "killing" us with? Could that explain "Christian" entertainment passing off as powerful Presence? Noise as anointing? Manipulation as wisdom? Predisposed response as glory? What do you think?

What I do know with absolute certainty is that this Jewish Fellow out of Bethlehem and Nazareth is the Guy who gutted the grave and hijacked hell. He heals the sick, cleanses lepers, raises the dead, and casts out devils—**and**—he passes on the power to his people to do the same and greater. He does not just put on a good show. We've been had! When Gentiles cut from the Jews, we cut from **The** Jew, and ended up with intellectually appealing, and thus "**traditionally** (**not** scripturally) sound" mirages mirroring the angel of light. That's what I think— and to the degree that we get back on God's master plan, which has Israel as his heart, to that same degree will we **experience** healing the sick, cleansing the lepers, raising the dead, casting out devils, and establishing a whole one new family to do the same. We could experience Abba back in his garden, "walking in the cool wind (Spirit) of the day."

Here's a Thought:

Do we think that because Israel messed up, and the **nation** did not enter into its destiny in the first century that God threw out the nation forever? Some think that. Some just haven't thought it out. To think it through gets scary. I mean, there have been times (notice the plural) that I really, **really** blew it big time. My **experience** has been that God did **not** throw **me** away forever, though sometimes it looked like he had, and I felt like he had. But, given time, God has **always managed somehow in his great love to turn me and bring me back**. I gotta believe he wouldn't do less for "Israel, his firstborn."

Here's a Question:

Who wants to do dumb? I don't want to do any more dumb! I've "done downright dumb." I don't want to "do dumb no mo'." Do you? I wish I could give you all 27 pages of these scriptures, but you can find them. As you search these out for yourself without "benefit" (ha) of "the church replaced Israel" spectacles, I promise this truth will jump out on you. God's love for Israel and the place he adamantly declares is theirs unconditionally will get all over you and all down through you. I'm telling you— "Christian" religion fitted me with demon eyeglasses—because I innocently trusted those who were "something" in the religion about me. God had to arrest me to fix my eyesight. I was taught wrong, led wrong, learned wrong, and nearly died wrong! I had an **amazing** experience about this thing.

Here's "What If":

What if Jeremiah and all these boys were true prophets and really did speak God's heart for Israel?

217

They said God would bring her back to the land.
"Okay. So God brought some of them back from
Babylon into the land way back there and that
fulfilled all those prophecies," someone may say.
That's how my thoughts used to run track. **Problem
is**—God had Jeremiah and the boys say that he
would bring them back, **and** set them back up on
their **very own and same dirt forever!** That did **not**
happen then. It's that "forever thing" that sprang on
me. **How** did the great scholars miss that for so
long? I mean, it's over and over and **over**. You have
to be brain dead to miss it, **once you throw away
those old anti-Jew eyeglasses**. You have to **deliberately** miss it—really handle the words and the text
wickedly not to see it. So what? Maybe God hides it
'till our heart's right? Can't tell, so can't say. **Can**
say I now see.

   What if God really does keep his blood
covenant with the nation of Israel?

   What if God really did orchestrate the formation
of this nation back about the time I graduated from
high school? Wonder if God could have kept me
(**and you**) all this time so I (we) could live to see
him take his blood-dirt back? **That's** a good, heavy
thought.

   What if God really is fighting for Israel like he
has been known to do?

   What if *God Himself* is **"on Israel's side?"**
Know what? This arresting encounter I experienced
says that's precisely the case. I'm not trying to come
across as a heavyweight theologian, but I did have a
little light flicker on, and I refuse to do a dumb-down

for my trail ahead. I refuse to ignore what and who God spotlights in his overall plan. I don't have to understand it to accept it. God loves the nation of Israel? Then I'm **crazy** about her—**love** the nation of Israel. I can do that without understanding details. Love doesn't demand 'em.

Giving lip service toward Israel and polishing up my Messianic vocabulary is **not, not, not** what I'm talking about. Love takes a stand—in God's plan. Love stands for peace, for shalom. Love stands for justice, for righteousness. Love **stands up**. I want to do that—write to do that. I **plan** to do that with all my strength and resources from here on into glory. I'm for the God of Abraham, Isaac, Jacob, King David and **The** King David getting their blood-dirt back. With power in the blood—**in Israel, the nation**—they get a chance to rule the world—forever. For me, doing otherwise at this stage would be a dumb-down. No more talking Jerusalem and walking Babylon, no mounting monuments of "ministries" independently skyward toward God, nor taking part in and admiring anyone who is. **I'm done with that deal!** 'Convinced I've been preserved till the time when Adonai's attention is turned onto his nation Israel, and his ear is hearing their cry. Count me in, Lord. I'm in for the long haul—all the way back to blood-dirt.

Here's Yeshua:

Talking to Nicodemus: "Nic, you have to go back to the drawing board, my friend. The religious system has built in so much ritualistic, blind-rote, programmed stuff that hearts are dark, cold, and hard—the whole nation divided. You and your people, the Jews, have just got to go all the way back into the Beginning—all the way back into Abba's heart, and come forth with a brand new start. I'm the only one who can take you there. You have to be birthed again from the beginning. The whole nation needs regeneration. **All of you** have to be born again from the beginning, including yourself, although you're a leader and a teacher. You've got to have a new heart. I'm here as the One who can take you and the whole nation back into Alpha—and this time we'll get it right. I'm the last Adam, now come to you as the Way back into Abba's garden-heart of love for you and the whole nation."

Jesus stood there as Amos' plumb line, ready to gather all into himself, and line it all back up according to Adonai's original specs. This side of the open tomb, he still stands, still ready, still speaking, still doing, one by one till all the temple's done. The way up in God is always to take the servant-down step. Only God lifts one up (and puts down another). The way forward in God is backward—back down that long plumb line through Plumb-line Messiah. The way into fullness is emptiness. The way to connect with God is to disconnect—disconnect with our own roots, our own ancestry, and connect through the Jewish Plumb-line to our Jewish roots, all the way back to our Father Abraham. This takes us through the nation of Israel (Jacob), back through Isaac, Abraham, Noah, Enoch, Abel, and past the flaming swords into Eden. There in Alpha, in Eden, we discover Omega, Jerusalem-above, now clothed on and one with Jerusalem-dirt-down.

Here's The Olive Tree:

It appears to be grafting time—but for whom? Grafting **back in** for Jews? I'm not sure. There's this "fullness of the Gentiles" thing. What does that mean? Whatever it means, it does **not** mean Gentiles all fragmented, fractured, fuming, fussing, fighting over figureheads, and foaming out frothy, lifeless nothingness. It does not mean competition, control, manipulation, building independent ministry empires, hawking giftings—all while God's chosen nation languishes in a death defying dragon confrontation. This woman-nation needs help through some love-weeping humans—some **bodies** filled with the resurrected body of the resurrected Jew who wept over this woman in the body he gave up for her.

Where are the churches and "movements of God" that are filled with the ultimate Lover? I've been made aware of a few, but not the "by and large." There's what—a billion "Christians?" I can see the few churches and ministries that are love-locked into helping the nation of Israel as being grafted into the cultivated olive tree. What about the rest of us? Are our churches grafted in? All these women, kids, babies, men—**people** just like us—getting blown into grotesque pieces week after week—**this** is the cultivated olive tree. Are our hearts grafted in, one with their hearts that pump blood out into the dirt?

The olive tree of Israel is getting chopped on, sawed on, blown up, blown about, blasted through, bombed out, starved, strangled, parched and pawed, raped, murdered, brutalized, assaulted and struck down. **(Sounds like The Holocaust to me!)** Where are the billion "Christians?" Are we grafted in? To what level of love can we claim to be grafted in? Is it deep enough **into the cultivated tree** for the graft to hold so our branch lives on God's tree?

How can we claim grafting in if we're going about our "wild olive tree" business of church as usual? How grafted in are we when we're building independent mega-churches, my way mega-ministries, mega-messes of machined "Christianity," going wilder and growing even wilder with no more than a passing prayer interest in the cultivated olive tree's welfare? How can we hear about bombed babies, scattered chunks of human flesh, and balls of blood-matted hair **week after week for years** without passionate travail tearing our guts out on behalf of the natural olive tree—**if** we're part of it—**if** we're grafted in? **Are** we part of it? Are we really grafted in? Are the Gentiles grafted in—in order for the cut off "Jew-branches" to be grafted **back** in? With our arrogant airs, could we be pushing God's frustration button?

Best I remember from science and agriculture classes in college, branches are vital to a strong tree trunk and root system. Seems like the leaves on the branches process something from the sun's energy that feeds the root system, which in turn, supports the branches. Something like that. Is that right? If so, wild olive branches **truly** grafted in completely could generate a growth spurt of the whole "old" tree. We can "hasten the Day of the Lord" by losing ourselves over into the passionate heart of Yeshua-Abba ("YeShAbba" See Glossary) **on behalf of the nation of Israel.** Our Father then can bring forth his own chosen nation Israel into their destiny of being **his** heart in earth to deliver or destroy at his heart's love-cry.

God's plan calls for a nation, a people, who will rise, and, in God's name, declare, "There shall be war no longer," and proceed with justice to make it stick throughout the earth. It **is** coming. It **is** written. This nation, held in the heart of the Lover God, will care zero for political correctness. **This** nation, "under God," will speak for God with his authority, "If you declare war, if you practice violence—on the orders of God, with angelic assistance, **we will kill you!** We are under unbreakable orders to **kill all killers.** The Prince of Peace, the King of Shalom is here to establish his rule of peace and love throughout all nations in creation." The nation regeneration is in process—under construction. Are **we** being grafted in? Lord, let it be! And let it hold!

CHAPTER 27

Coming Out of the "Male-box"

———➤◦◄———

"God has no gender?" Okay. I can handle that—sort of. "God is 100 percent male?" (as I recently read?) **Now**, I have a problem—no "sort of" to it. I just flat-out have a problem—unless we can add to that "God is 100 percent female." Then I'm within my handling capacity again. You've already read about my problem with all the "**born** again" business without **any** femininity present whatsoever. Just can't figure it. Maybe my "handler" lost a handle somewhere and it's gouged me in the head. Maybe I've seen one woman too many spiritually male-molested out of her inheritance in the name of God with a submission stick and a macho-god trick.

I don't know—but here we go. You really don't have to follow, you know. You can just ease the lid back down on the good-old-boy's god-box, and do your best to hold God in the malebox. I don't think you'll be able to do it at this late day, but if you're so driven, I guess you'll just have to try—**without** me. I gave it up. Saw too many bleached bones of the blue-bloods who tried it. Too many crusades—too many holocausts—too many mule-headed men mumbling something about men's houses being their castles, and "God put **me** in charge of the universe." And **look at the condition of the universe after 10,000 years! Men's** traditions are **much** more treasured by some than others.

To the few willing to break out of the malebox: Can it get worse? You think so? Well, at least, let it get worse, with us **trying** in faith-works to make it better. Let's do **something** from God about the mess that's different than what we've **been** doing forever. (And some man just said, "What mess? Everything's fine. My wife **knows her place** and she's happy. Isn't that right, honey?" "Yes dear," she says, and when he looks away, she rolls her eyes—**again**.) Let's **change**.

El Shadday

I did a double take about a year ago while listening to Christian radio: **"the many breasted One?"** Did I hear **that**? I waited. Yep, they sang it again. "Wow," I thought, "I best look into that." One of the names for God is "El Shadday," usually translated from the Hebrew as "Almighty." Strong's Hebrew and Greek Dictionary traces it back to a root word "shad" which is "probably from H7736 (in its original sense) contracted; the **breast** of a woman or animal (as **bulging**):—**breast, pap, teat**." O-o-o-o-kay.

To Brood

Strong says this Hebrew word (H7363) is from a primitive root which means "**to brood**; by implication **to be relaxed:—flutter, move, shake**." Brown-Driver-Briggs definition is: (Qal) **to grow soft, relax**; (Piel) **to hover**. The word appears early on, in Genesis 1:2, "The earth was without form, and void; and darkness *was* on the face of the deep. And the Spirit of God was **hovering** (or brooding) over the face of the waters." (NKJV) The word is also used in Deuteronomy 32:10, 11, "As an eagle stirs up its nest, **hovers** over its young, spreading out its wings, taking them up, carrying them on its wings. . . ., and in Jeremiah 23:9, "Concerning the prophets: My heart is broken within me; all my bones **tremble**."

I looked up "brood" in Webster: as a verb, it means: "**to sit on eggs so as to hatch** them." To throw in a couple o' freebies: "brood-mare (noun). A mare kept for **breeding** purposes." A "brooder" (is) "a heated device for **rearing** chicks artificially." So forms of the English word in modern usage are associated with "breeding" and "rearing" offspring. Hmmm. Again, "In the beginning God created the heavens and the earth. Now the earth was formless and empty, darkness was over the surface of the deep, and **the Spirit of God was hovering over** (or **brooding over**) the waters." (See Gen 1:1, 2)

This is **not** hard for me: A part of the Creator, the Spirit of God, is hovering in a brooding way "to sit on (these) eggs (in this deep, dark water-nest) so as to hatch them." A part of God is brooding over this formless emptiness to birth out of it what's been put in this nest. Sounds to me like **she's** sitting on the nest for **him** in a joint venture. They're in this beginning-thing together. However, I **did** have to get past trying to fit this and other like-scriptures into the pre-set, all-male-God box—had to get willing for the real Brooder that bred me and birthed me to rear me—alongside Abba. Then I found myself in a **large** place before God. Mysteries began to unfold as Abba and Brooder raised me on hidden manna from heaven. I got so heaven-hungry I didn't even notice who all agreed (really didn't care). I just ate sweet cakes and meat steaks and kept on growing and going. I didn't have time to argue for eating. Seems now I have to write while I eat. I'm **happy**, I'm eating—and writing. Somebody may read it some day and go, "Ah-h-h, **wait just a minute**. Let me read that again. I think that made sense." Shoot, I can't half explain what I eat anyway—be like trying to explain the shortbread cookies DeDe feeds me. I don't try; I just eat—and make those "um-huh" sounds.

We'll never travel if we don't get moving. When we headed out for Malibu and the ocean once, we spotted it on the map first. Let's spot our destination at Revelation 12. (**Read it please**.) Once we watched the wide water a while in Malibu, we got adventuresome from there. We may do that when we've been around the Wonder Woman in Revelation 12 a while. I've been noticing her having a hard time for a **long** time. Something about a nice Lady in distress that gets my attention and moves me to help her. She reminds me of the Brooder Lady back there in Genesis. I think Brooder was in love with her husband and really "putting herself at risk" to make him happy. Who can help admiring a woman like that? I think this could be Brooder here again in Rev 12—or some of her kin.

Brooder in Genesis was **big,** to be brooding over the whole mass of creation. This one in Rev 12 is big—**look** at her. She's dressed in the **sun** and standing on the **moon** with twelve of the main **stars** shining in her hair. What a wardrobe—what a woman! **Who's** woman is she? Who's her husband? I wonder. Got to be the same woman, don't you think? Talk about big and beautiful—she is. Ever see a woman who's had twelve kids and **still** looks good? I think this woman's been giving birth **ever since Genesis.** And she's still beautiful. But who **is** she? Who **is** she? You won't quit reading if I tell you? Shhh—whisper it. (She's God.) Don't go yelling it now to a bunch o' folks. They'll jump all over you. Why? Because, obviously, this is a female, "and **everybody** knows God is male." See what I'm saying? You've got to be cool about this. It's a mystery—been hidden—and the time may not quite be here yet for the many, but it is for the few. That includes you (or you wouldn't still be reading). She's God—not **all** of God, but **all-God**—God 100 percent female—**and**—100 percent male. Yes, I know: "In Christ there is not male and female (no "plumbing" required)." But God created mankind in his likeness, and mankind is male and female so **somewhere** in God there is male and female. If it's not in Christ, the Son, it must be in the Son's Father and Mother, Christ's Parent(s). (They're all One in a "3-thru" Unit.) I'd like to take you on a guided tour between Genesis one and Revelations twelve, stopping off briefly at some historic spots here and there. I'll share with you what I've learned from previous visits, and you can explore them on your own.

Word in Creation (See Genesis 1 and Proverbs 8 and 9.):

God brought forth his inner Self as his fellow Creator to work alongside him, one with him, in all his creativity and shaping. He calls her (this inner Self), "Wisdom" (English), or "Sophia" (Greek). He spoke Word (Yeshua) to the dark waters; she had the waters covered, so she received Word into her blanket, and Abba pressed Word, held in the blanket, on down into the deep formless matter. (Like putting a cloth over a glass, placing a seed in the cloth, and pressing the cloth, with the seed inside, **down into** the glass. Although the seed is in the cloth, it is also in the glass. When it sprouts and grows, you can "bring forth" the seed by pulling the cloth up out of the glass.) Sophia carried Word in her womb, that was submerged into the deep, until Word "grew" to accomplish that particular part of creation that Abba had in mind when he spoke. This process was repeated over and over and over all through creation as the God-Family worked together, One, in the creative process until the creating was done. When

Abba brought forth Eve **from inside** Adam, he was revealing this image of himself, with herself resting one inside him—yet able to be brought forth to work be-side him.

Word in Egypt: (See Exodus 7-14)

Israel cried out and God heard. Sophia blanketed the people and God spoke Word down toward the people. Sophi's blanket held Word and Abba pressed him in among the people through Moses, Aaron, Miriam, and others. Sophi used him to bring the nation out through the Red Sea birth canal and a nation was born.

Word in Virgin Mary (See Luke 1)

The angel answered, (1) "The Holy Spirit will come upon you, **and** (2) the power of the Most High will overshadow you. So (3) the holy one to be born will be called the Son of God. . ." (Luke 1:35) Sophia came upon Mary—blanketed her—and Abba's presence was over her to place the Seed of Christ into her. Sophi received the Seed into **her** blanket-womb and Abba pressed Seed, still in the blanket, into Mary's womb. Mary was carrying Christ **inside of Spirit's womb** which was inside of Mary's womb. (Remember again the seed wrapped in the cloth and pressed inside the glass 'til time for it to come out, still in the cloth.) Sophia was pregnant with Jesus—inside Mary's physical womb. Jesus was being held in the Spirit-womb which was lining Mary's womb. When time was up, Abba pulled the cloth out, the cloth still holding Seed-Son, and Mary called him Yeshua—he shall save his people from their sins, just like he saved Israel out of Egypt.

Word in Males and Females (See Luke 1)

Again, The angel answered, (1) "The Holy Spirit will come upon you, **and** (2) the power of the Most High will overshadow you. So (3) the holy one to be born will be called the Son of God." (Luke 1:35) He shall save his people from their sins. How? John 16:8, "When he (the Counselor) comes, he will convict the world (and individuals in it) of guilt in regard to sin and righteousness and judgment." Yeshua-Abba (one) brings (or sends) Counselor. (Careful study reveals "Counselor" to be—yes—the Holy Spirit, **but** the Holy Spirit love-fused-one with Father-Son—the **full load** of Godhood— "YeShAbba." See "Glossary.") Counselor "sits down over" and commences conviction in the deep-most spirit part of a person. When the person yields to the Spirit's blanket-covering, Abba ("part" of Counselor), presses Seed-Son ("part" of Counselor) **into the Spirit-blanket** that is covering and on **down into the spirit** of the repentant person. Jesus is **in Sophia's womb** which is being carried now **inside the believer.** The seed, Jesus, has been placed in the cloth (Spirit-blanket), and pressed down inside the jar (believer's spirit.) Sophia now "carries" Jesus in her womb inside the believer to full term—till Jesus can be birthed out **through believer**, making believer one with Jesus in the process. He is "Christ in you, the hope of glory."

That is, Christ in you is the hope God has of his glory coming out through you, so that when he appears out through you, you appear in the glory, one with him.

Word in The World (See John 16)

But I tell you the truth: It is for your good that **I am going away**. Unless I go away, the Counselor will not come to you; but if I go, I will send him to you. [8]When he comes, he will **convict the world** (as a whole as well as persons in it) of guilt– in regard to sin and righteousness and judgment: [9]in regard to sin, because men do not believe in me; [10]in regard to righteousness, because I am going to the Father, where you can see me no longer. (John 16:7-10) Yeshua had entered **physically** into the world through Mary. He was getting ready to leave **physically**. He knew Abba was close to "pulling the Seed out of the glass" and bringing him out of the world he entered through the womb of Mary. God was about to "bow the heavens and come down" again as the prophet had cried. This happened at the crucifixion when God turned out the lights after Jesus cried, "It's **done**, Abba!" Father inhaled up inside himself his Son's Spirit—up into his swallowing-up fire, and the Godhood metamorphosed into a glorified human-God-flesh, "housing" the glory-merged Abba-Son **in** Holy Spirit—a new "3-Thru" (See "Glossary") Creation, with characteristics and capabilities never before possessed—like John saw on Patmos—**in the Spirit**. One capability is the possibility of this 3-thru GodMates-creature having adaptations-capability so as to **enter** mortals in this heavenly fire **without** making instant "burnt-being" out of 'em. This is who enters when a person believes and receives Christ into his or her spirit-life. Believer gets to "eat" the "full meal-deal" of heaven into his or her life. That's Person to person, but there is a "yet once more" bowing down of the heavens that will blanket (or has already blanketed) the planet and rumble a fire throughout creation. The **world** will come under blanketing like never experienced. Sophia will settle her cover on down, the world around—like dropping a bed blanket on a coconut, so thorough will be the covering. The whole creation groans and travails under this. Conviction will be **smothering** under the mothering. Only way of escape will be out through Sophi's Son. She won't let you wiggle any other way. She will hold the world in her womb, carry it walking wide-legged and suffering 'til Abba says, "It's delivery time." Then she'll "give it up" to him. It'll be like Israel coming through the Red Sea to be birthed as a nation. Only this time, she's not just "carrying" one nation. She's got her belly full of creation and "about nine months gone," walking around in a **bad** neighborhood. A woman just ought not get **caught** there, but she did. She chooses to live here till Hubby pulls the heaven-cloth up out of the world-glass and a "new baby world" is born.

The Rev 12 Lady

[1]A great and wondrous sign appeared in heaven: a woman clothed with the sun, with the moon under

her feet and a crown of twelve stars on her head. [2]She was pregnant and cried out in pain as she was about to give birth. [3]Then another sign appeared in heaven: an enormous red dragon. . . . The dragon stood in front of the woman who was about to give birth, so that he might devour her child the moment it was born. [5]**She gave birth** to a son, a male child, who will rule all the nations with an iron scepter. And her child was snatched up (raptured up) to God and to his throne. [6]The woman fled into the desert to a place prepared for her by God, where she might be taken care of for 1,260 days. (See Rev 12:1-6)

True, this male son is Yeshua ("Christ **in** you, the hope of glory)." **But**, this is not **just** Yeshua coming forth from the womb of the Virgin Mary. **Earlier**, he came into the world that way, made his sacrifice, became one with Abba in the heavenly fires of love, and then descended back into the world at Pentecost. Sophia had covered those gathered, Abba had pressed Yeshua into her blanket and **on inside each one's spirit**, not into physical wombs like he was in Mary. Now Mary, along with whoever else would choose to do so all down through history, could receive into her **spirit** the Seed she had earlier received into her **womb**. **Think of what a joy payment** that must have been to the mother who had watched and felt all his pain, suffering and rejection—and **seeming** total failure! Think of the joy that overflowed the heart of her son, Yeshua. God, you are **awesome**—and faithful beyond my imagination!

Oh! But this mystery has **multiple** dimensions,

including the following prophetic pictures. (1) A picture of Father Mothering Jesus out of Mary's womb by Holy Spirit, (2) a prophetic picture of Father Mothering Son from his wife, Israel, of whom Mary was part, by Holy Spirit, (3) a prophetic picture of Father Mothering **all of creation to come forth as a new creation-creature** by Holy Spirit. The "womb of the morning," the new age, is Holy Spirit. She "pulls seed" from Jews and Gentiles—Israel and the church for this birth.

Let's look down into this mystery a moment. This male son, Jesus, **glorified now into YeShAbba,** has been "implanted" into "spirit-wombs" the world over. This Rev 12 Sophia woman is screaming for Hubby to "pull" all of her Son's "body parts" on **out of her birth canal that stretches from her womb in earth all the way up into the heavens.** She is really in trouble with this long and impeded birth canal. She's giving every contraction all she's got, but **she's not dilating** enough for this world-sized womb-dweller to come forth. She's got all kinds of backache, bellyache, gas pains, heartburn, swelling—all the built-in, "baby-house" complications—and that's the **good** news! With every contraction getting harder, she's facing an **outside** foe worse than the inside woe. At the bottom of her enormous belly, belching his threatening breath all over her, gloating in her agonizing suffering, stands the monster of monsters, **ready to eat her baby** when he comes out—**before** he can rise to rule the world.

Sophia closed her eyes and looked ahead to see

the fruit of her labor. She remembered "the Jerusalem that is above is **free**, and **she is our mother**." (Gal 4:26) Her thoughts turned to Jerusalem above and she saw a new heaven and a new earth, for the first heaven and the first earth had passed away, and there was no longer any sea. **She saw the Holy City, the new Jerusalem, coming down out of heaven from God, prepared as a bride beautifully dressed for her husband.** She heard a loud voice from the throne saying, **"Now the dwelling of God is with men, and he will live with them**. They will be his people, and **God himself will be with them and be their God.** He will wipe every tear from their eyes. **There will be no more** death or **mourning or crying or pain**, for the old order of things has passed away.

He who was seated on the throne said, "**I am making everything new!" These words are trustworthy and true.**" She heard: "**It is done**. I am the Alpha and the Omega, the Beginning and the End. To him who is thirsty I will give to drink without cost from the spring of the water of life. He who overcomes will inherit all this, and I will be his God and he will be my son.

One of the seven angels said, "**Come, I will show you the bride, the wife of the Lamb.**" And he carried me away in the Spirit to a mountain great and high, and showed me the Holy City, Jerusalem, **coming down out of heaven from God**. It shone with the glory of God, and its brilliance was like that of a very precious jewel, like a jasper, clear as crystal. It had a great, high wall with twelve gates, and with twelve angels at the gates. On the gates were written the names of the twelve tribes of Israel. There were three gates on the east, three on the north, three on the south and three on the west. The wall of the city had twelve foundations, and on them were the names of the twelve apostles of the Lamb.

The city's wall was made of jasper, and the city of pure gold, as pure as glass. The foundations of the city walls were decorated with every kind of precious stone. The first foundation was jasper, the second sapphire, the third chalcedony, the fourth emerald, the fifth sardonyx, the sixth carnelian, the seventh chrysolite, the eighth beryl, the ninth topaz, the tenth chrysoprase, the eleventh jacinth, and the twelfth amethyst. The twelve gates were twelve pearls, each gate made of a single pearl. The great street of the city was of pure gold, like transparent glass.

I did not see a temple in the city, because the Lord God Almighty and the Lamb are its temple. The city does not need the sun or the moon to shine on it, for the glory of God gives it light, and the Lamb is its lamp. **The nations will walk by its light, and the kings of the earth will bring their splendor into it.** On no day will its gates ever be shut, for there will be no night there. The glory and honor of the nations **will be brought into it**. **Nothing impure will ever enter it, nor will anyone who does what is shameful or deceitful,** but only those whose names are written in the Lamb's book of life. (See Revelations 21)

She could see and hear all this. She was strengthened by the joy set before her. She saw where the nations and kings **would** be brought into it and she **knew** her Husband would make it so. She could not fail. She would not fail. "Nothing impure, no one who does shameful, deceitful stuff?" Why, that meant that, for the dragon, it was but a matter of time. **He could not enter**. Since this was Husband-Son City, this was **her** city. "In fact," she said to herself, "**I AM** the city—**I AM** the Mother of it all. It is finished already; I will labor 'til I birth in the earth what's been made mine.

Sophi's final labor pains are to deliver Abba's **creation in its entirety** back up to him for his own good pleasure. These are but a few of the contractions she's still caught in:

- Bride nation Israel crying out in the womb of the morning to be delivered into her destiny.
- Bride church, scattered, and crying out for gathering into oneness with mother nation Israel.
- Individuals crying out in darkness to be delivered over into the kingdom of light.
- Nations crying out in fear of extinction to be liberated into new Jerusalem.
- The whole creation reeling under man's rebellion, groaning for new birthing.
- **Abba's** burning desire for his new earth order; he wants his wife and garden back.
- **Abba's** yearning for males in his new order to be revealing himself in the new earth.
- **Abba's** craving for females in his new order to be revealing Sophia in the new earth.
- **Abba's** burning desire for male and female to be

one flesh in his new earth order.

♦ **Abba's** burning desire for his and Sophia's Song of Songs depth of passion to be lived out in regenerated flesh of husbands and wives in his new earth order.

♦ **Abba's** burning desire for oneness with his creation—for oneness of Christ and the church to **contribute** to oneness of the church and Israel—for oneness of husband-wife marital passion to **contribute** to this oneness with him.

♦ **Paul's** still crying out: "Therefore, I **urge you**, brothers: **offer your bodies** as living sacrifices. **Do not conform any longer—be transformed**." (See Romans 12:1, 2)

Read here in this one little chapter of Romans 8 and get a tiny glimpse of love contractions required for creation transformation. Holy Spirit is the only One powerful enough to **agonize** in the pain of "planet-child" birth until full delivery into Father's heart and plan. I've marked some obvious "love contractions required" (LCR) workings: I consider that our present sufferings are not worth comparing with the glory that **will be revealed** in us (through love contractions of the Holy Spirit). The creation waits in eager expectation for the sons of God **to be revealed**. (LCR) For the creation was subjected to frustration, not by its own choice, but by the will of the one who subjected it, in hope that the creation itself will be liberated from its bondage to decay and **brought into** the glorious freedom of the children of God (LCR).

We know that **the whole creation has been groaning as in the pains of childbirth right up to the present time** (LCR). Not only so, but **we ourselves,** who have the firstfruits of the Spirit, **groan inwardly** (LCR) as we wait eagerly for our adoption as sons, the redemption of our bodies (LCR). For in this hope we were saved. But hope that is seen is no hope at all. Who hopes for what he already has? But if we hope for what we do not yet have, we wait for it patiently (LCR).

In the same way, **the Spirit helps us in our weakness** (LCR). We do not know what we ought to pray for, but the Spirit himself intercedes for us with groans that words cannot express (LCR). And he who searches our hearts knows the mind of the Spirit, because the Spirit intercedes for the saints in accordance with God's will (LCR) And we know that in all things **God works** (LCR) for the good of those who love him, who have been called according to his purpose. [29]For those God foreknew he also predestined **to be conformed to the likeness of his Son** (LCR), that he might be the firstborn among many brothers. (LCR) And those he predestined, he also called; those he called, he also justified (LCR); those he justified, he also glorified. (LCR)

What, then, shall we say in response to this? If God is for us, who can be against us? He who did not spare his own Son, but gave him up for us all—how will he not also, along with him, graciously give us all things? (LCR) Who will bring any charge against those (LCR) whom God has chosen? It is God who justifies. (LCR) Who is he that condemns?

(LCR) Christ Jesus, who died—more than that, who was raised to life—is at the right hand of God and is also interceding for us (LCR). Who shall separate us (LCR) from the love of Christ? Shall trouble (LCR) or hardship (LCR) or persecution (LCR) or famine (LCR) or nakedness (LCR) or danger (LCR) or sword? (LCR) As it is written: "For your sake we face death all day long; (LCR) we are considered as sheep to be slaughtered." (LCR)

No, in all these things we are more than conquerors through him who loved us. For I am convinced that neither death (LCR) nor life (LCR) , neither angels (LCR) nor demons (LCR), neither the present (LCR) nor the future (LCR) nor any powers (LCR), neither height (LCR) nor depth (LCR), nor anything else in all creation (LCR), will be able to separate us (LCR) from the love of God that is in Christ Jesus our Lord.

Love contractions are required for all of this, and **we** don't have the strength for it. It has to be done **for** us by the Spirit over us, in us, through us, and around us. I **love** this Woman! Is it any wonder the dragon is blowing his rotten, terrifying breath on her? Look at all she's carrying! Any wonder "she screamed in the agony of labor?" (Stern's CJB) Abba, get some of us "birthed on out" to stand and identify with **you** so we can stand guard and let you use us to doctor, nurse, serve, and **cooperate with this Woman's labor.**

CHAPTER 28

WW II—World War Rages Around Two Women

A Shocker for Sure

Women are up-front on the end-time battle lines. (Two women in The Revelation 12, 17) Let's look **false** first: Think **9-1-1**. How were those young men motivated? These are excerpts from an article in "The New York Times" September 29, 2001, by Gustav Niebuhr, "Injunctions to Pray, Instructions to Kill" (Letter to the Hijackers)

"Also, do not seem confused or show signs of nervous tension. Be happy, optimistic, calm, because you are heading for a deed that God loves and will accept [as a good deed]. It will be the day, God willing, you spend **with the women of paradise.** Smile in the face of hardship young man/For you are heading toward eternal paradise.

"Know that **the gardens of paradise** are waiting for you in all their beauty, **and the women of paradise are waiting, calling out, "Come hither, friend of God." They have dressed in their most beautiful clothing.**

"Check your weapon before you leave and long before you leave. (You must make your knife sharp and you must not discomfort your animal during the **slaughter**).

"If God decrees that any of you are to **slaughter**, you should dedicate the **slaughter** to your fathers and [unclear], because you have obligations toward them. Do not disagree, and obey. If you **slaughter**, do not cause the discomfort of those you are killing,

"Then implement the way of the prophet in taking prisoners. Take prisoners and kill them. As Almighty God said: **"No prophet should have prisoners until he has soaked the land with blood…"**

The more they soak the land with blood, **the more women they are promised in the gardens of paradise.** False paradise, false promise to be sure— but a true fact—that the false promise **is** held out by the enraged demon of violence, terror, and war. Women are a big part of the luscious bait on Satan's hellish hook.

"Jews & Blues" is working on **Gan-Eden, the true (not** Islamic) **Garden of Eden Paradise**, revealed to us as the dream of Abba (**not** allah)—of Abraham, Isaac (**not** Ishmael)—of Jacob (**not** Esau)—of David, and Yeshua (**not** Mohammed). That's just to keep the record straight.

Who's Your Woman?

Would you help the writer out a little here? Thanks! Open your Bible to Revelation, chapters 12 and 17 for this "World War." It's the story of two women at war for the world. Let's give them names—"Sophi" is into birthing, "Babbi" into battling—Sophi's in dire distress, Babbi's in drunkenness. Look at 'em: **Sophi** is in Revelation 12 (I use NRSV here.) She's in **hard** labor, but hanging in there. **Babbi** is in Revelation 17 (NRSV): "[1]Then one of the seven angels who had the seven bowls came and said to me, Come, I will show you the judgment of **the great whore who is seated on many waters. I saw a woman sitting on a scarlet beast.** [4]The woman was clothed in purple and scarlet, and adorned with gold and jewels and pearls, holding in her hand a golden cup full of abominations and the impurities of her fornication; [5]and on her forehead was written a name, a mystery: "Babylon the great (false religious system), **mother of whores** and **(mother) of earth's abominations**." [6]And I saw that **the woman was drunk** with the blood of the saints and the blood of the witnesses to Jesus. (Her favorite label? **"Believer Blood**.") The waters that you saw, where the (drunk) whore is seated, are **peoples and multitudes and nations and languages**. [16]And the ten horns that you saw, they "and" the beast (a better translation is "that you saw **'upon'** the beast") will hate the (drunk) whore; they (the ten horns) will make her desolate and naked; **they will devour her flesh and burn her up with fire**. [17]For God has put it into their hearts to carry out his purpose by agreeing to give their kingdom to the beast, **until** the words of God will be fulfilled. [18]**The (drunk) woman you saw is the great city (Babylon) that rules over the kings of the earth.**" (She's **really** into control—and crazy drunk.)

So here are the two women—both out in the desert—one drunk and one distressed. One dressed up, dressed out lavishly and loaded in loot, the other exposed in the helpless state of giving birth, laboring with her whole heart for all she's worth. Which camp are we in? There are no others. It's show-time. This is the showdown war for God's creation. Both women are "user-friendly." Sophi is married, being used by her Husband to birth a new "baby." Babbi is user-friendly with a Beast, a beastly nature. Her legs are spread wide for the ride, Sophi's are spread for delivery. Each woman has given herself to someone else. Neither is acting alone—each is "under the influence" of another. Is this **really** war for the whole creation that's groaning in labor for the manifestation of the sons of God? Surely it must be.

Background

Let's go back to the beginning in the Garden of Eden—back to mankind being created in God's image. His image is Family. So, out of the entire creation (including church **in** Israel—church **and** Israel), what does God aim to get? What is the Creator-Gardener's Wife birthing? Offspring, children—to form a **full** family.

So the whole creation is groaning, Israel is

moaning, and the whole true church body is caught up in turmoil of labor. God is after what he's been after all along—a family of one-with-God creatures in his creation. The focus is on family. God wants his family in his garden. God created family "in his image and in his likeness." Family was heart to the whole creation.

Babbi's camp is not a family camp; it is a spiritual death-camp, full of folk in the drunk-blind state of confusion about God's destiny for their lives. They're dressed up drunk on independent self-gratification, accompanying customized religion, with intellectually rationalized justification. They're riding what looks and feels like a safe "easy pony," but inside the pony's hide lurks the wild beast nature of run-away Adam. He does not give a hoot-owl's holler about God's broken heart for his wayward children.

Is there church in Babbi's camp? Oh absolutely! Built on and backed up by Mighty Babylon. Programmed just to please your little heart, honey! Just to appease your conscience—"bring your family on by here, pay God some dues on the way to doing your own 'do's': Everything's gonna be all right; just you wait and see." But, even if God breaks into Babbi's camp for a bit, and you get something from him there, Babbi's loose-living lifestyle plan will **keep you from getting it to work when you get back home.** Don't be fooled! **Whatever** you're getting in church, and **however** much of God is there, as long as you're just doing God **in church**, Satan's sipping spiked-sodas with Babbi, and singing inside. He's not bothered by you one bit. **As long as God's not growing family, he's not worried.**

Start "taking church" home to your family and "doing God" at home, and you're headed into **Sophi's** family camp. You could learn how to merge your family in with God's. **Then** Smutty's bothered, nervous. He'll call for his home boys: "Party-gal time! Spruce her up, boys, and set her down, over there on the corner of Elm and Brown (or whatever your neighborhood is)." He's not really upset yet, since he's always been able to butt in on God's family and block out the blessing with something from his designer bag of delectable dainties and demonic devices. The whole family's not on fire yet so he's not frantic. He'll get 'em some free computer games installed or send 'em a bargain on a zillion channel TV dish with a fancier remote control and soon smother this little flame. No problem! It's the **family** on fire that sends him stomping on down the street.

The Big Loser

To understand Babbi, the beautiful, drunk whore (how a woman can be drunk and beautiful is itself a mystery to me), you think **spiritual** relations, not sex stuff. The sex setting is to get the point across about **very intimate** spiritual relations. Think idolatry, not sexual co-habitation. Think about shacking with demons, not topless dancers. Think un-holy spiritual relationship, not un-married sexual relations. Think disloyalty to God, not disloyalty to morality. Think "instead of" Christ, not "instead of chastity." Think "kingdom of God **not**-first" instead of "legal spouse not-first." Think about choosing not to love God with your whole heart, rather than about choosing not to love your sex-mate with all your heart. Think failure to serve pleasure to the Lord your God, rather than failure to serve sex only to your physical partner. Think unfaithfulness in your God relationship, not unfaithfulness in your marriage relationship. This is spiritual, not sexual. This is about the great whore of false, faked up, in-place-of-true-relationship-with-God **religion**, so beautifully organized, programized, plagiarized, popularized, polarized, de-sensitized, and mesmerized as **to take your spirit away from the living God.** Babbi is the great Babylon whore, beautiful to look at and easy to score. Just open up your **spirit** and she's there for more. **Warning**: AIDS is **nothing** compared to what "easy Babbi" is spreading. She unloads an **eternal** infection on you when you lay with her.

Thing is, Babbi sits on a wild beast that **only pretends** to let her be in control. The animal is wild and savage—not a nice, well trained, Tennessee Walker easy-rider. This is a beast under the influence all right, but not under **her** influence. There's a dragon down in there, out of sight, that this beast answers to. Queen-dressed Babbi is **absolutely and totally controlled and manipulated by the dragon through the beast beneath her.**

Babbi's deep-down beast nature that is fronted with fancy beauty and famous appearance has not been processed into Creator's patented regeneration plan. Sophi, on the other hand, lies helplessly laboring—completely caught up in processing. She's clothed with the Sun, the "owner" of the sky, and yields totally to his love. She is not in position to show off right now like Babbi's doing. She's lost herself to creation processing, dangerously giving herself away to Abba's heart.

The Big Lady

Give me the Rev 12 lady any day! Never mind her being proportionately out of shape right now. I can deal with that. I love this lady—and all who do the same. Blessed be the real holy lady. This is **not** the virgin Mary, but it **is** a crying shame that Mary, the mother of Jesus, has taken such a bum rap. **Such** a shame. What a lady herself. Yielding to this lady to come down upon her, yielding to the Most High who then overshadowed her to place his Seed within her body so that later he could be placed in her spirit and life—and in ours. What a lady and what an enduring pioneer through all her lifetime. So worthy of honor and credit for her trust, her yielding and her obedience in the face of uncertainty, ridicule, and persecution. What a woman! She gave herself to the regenerating process as a true pioneer of the faith. "Thank you, Mary" is what I will say to her when I see her. May the desert of this old unregenerate flesh of humankind be filled with women like her— yielded and under the influence of the big lady to "process the hell" out of God's people and get rid of Babbi in the deal.

This big lady birthed her Firstborn up to God and to his throne but she herself was given wings to fly to a place prepared in the wilderness desert of humankind—in the barren wasteland cultures of the condemned creation. While the dragon went off to make war with her seed, she flew off into a Papa-prepared place. There he could love her, protect her, and provide power for her to pull her scattered, unregenerate seed into her womb of the morning. There in her womb (Papa's heart), she could hold them for the patented process of regeneration to change them—individually and collectively, and birth the new earth to fit the new heaven.

The Big Liar

When it was all over, the dragon had to be terribly frustrated. He had stood right in front of the woman when she had her legs spread to deliver her baby. (How embarrassing to such a lovely, agonizing lady!) He was poised as The Snatcher, his breath in her face taunting her. He was all set, and she knew it—to **eat** her baby as soon as it came out, and jump on top of her to humiliate her in this vulnerable condition. What a beast! What would you think if this were your wife?

Liar beast got fooled. The male child came out, **but as a full grown man!** Liar went berserk—dropped in shock. **What?** How can this be? He blustered around; now **he's** under an Influence! He missed the offspring—the child having been caught up to God and his throne. Beast stewed and spewed, but **"the earth helped the woman."** How? By opening its mouth and **swallowing** what the dragon spewed out of his mouth." We can read about the earth swallowing up people outside the tabernacle of Moses when some of his folks went over the spewing limit— **big earthquake!** Earth opened up and swallowed **thousands** of people—not a trace of 'em found. "The earth" today is empowered in the mercy of God to use God's principles to swallow up religious stupidity infecting his creation. Go God Go!

Sophi is pregnant today with **"those who obey God's commandments and hold to the testimony of Jesus."** These in the earth are held in her womb, Father's heart, while God regenerates them into his image and likeness. Messiah Jesus, the exact image of God, swallowed up God's enemies on the cross, dragon-liar included, just before he committed himself to his consuming-fire Father—**enemies on fire ever since**. That helped the earth so the earth could help the woman. Now these "images and likenesses" of God "who obey God's commandments and hold to the testimony of Jesus" can do a little swallowing themselves in "The Name" that's above every name—in heaven and earth. They can swallow up beast to help the Lady birth. You see, she has birthed, is birthing, and will birth—like was, is, and is to come—like was saved, is being saved, and will be saved—an enduring process, patented in heaven. Takes big Lady and big labor to birth a little planet! She needs all the pushing help she can get. Let's empty the Babbi camp, cross over to Sophi and help her. What do you say?

CHAPTER 29

The Playoff

---※─◦─◦─※---

For as long as anyone could remember, the Rebels had ruled as Stupor Bowl champions. Their dynasty was unbroken, going back to when the game was played on dirt with no protective gear or uniforms. Why should this game be any different? They had their champagne stacked for the wild, post-game party. Final seconds: Rebels by 3. The Burners were bunched up back under their own goal posts. The Rebels were really roused—partying on the field; they could taste the bubbles—but the party didn't happen.

Quarterback Yeshua broke huddle—crowd roar was deafening. Down on the field, you could hear the Rebels cursing and calling: "Hey **Jew**-boy! Let's have it! What **happened** to all that big, bad, Burner fire—**Jew**-baby?" Others taunted in unison "**Jew**-baby, **Jew**-boy—**Jew**-baby, **Jew**-boy." With all the noise, Yeshua had to motion signals to his scraggly looking, scrappy little team. Quarterback sneak? Yeshua back-pedaled to the end zone marker. He cradled the ball near his heart, then straightened up, looked up—and—**out of nowhere** a whirlwind hit him. His body became a blur as he spun forward— **right up the middle**. His outstretched right arm sent mighty Rebels flying backwards like tilted dominos. In a second, he whirled across the goal line. The big game board flashed "Burners 6—Rebels 3." The game was over, the dynasty broken, the stands wild. That was last season; this is another. Here are some recordings from this season's big game:

First half: Rebels scored in the first quarter, but unsportsmanlike conduct nullified the play. Penalties plagued the Rebels throughout the quarter. The Burners went scoreless in the first half, but managed to hold the Rebels. They had help from the wind on the last play of the half when the Rebels went for an easy field goal. Wind had not been a factor, but, at the last second, a sudden gust blew the ball outside the uprights.

Halftime: talk was frantic. Fights broke out in the stands. Violence was in the air as storm clouds gathered. Halftime show was canceled and viewers all over the world were furious. The whole world was turned on and tuned in. Looking at the broadcasting booths, you saw interpreters sending the game to all nations. Michael and Gabriel at halftime:

Michael: Who could have dreamed these Burner rookies could have held the Rebels scoreless without any of last season's championship dream-team?

Gabriel: Not me, Michael. Everybody thought

when the champs went on strike for more money and walked out on the owner that the Burners would fold. The owner said, "No way! We'll find some rookies who'll play their hearts out 'til our champs come back. The Champs love the game; they're just not thinking straight now—but they will. We're still a winning team. We're still contenders, and we'll still take the Rebels in The Stupor Bowl." He placed great confidence in these rookies he found, Mike, and I've got to think he's pleased with 'em so far.

Michael: These Burner rookies made a lot of mistakes, but they played with reckless abandon and a team unity seldom seen. "Can they go the distance with that same intensity?" is the question. They're giving away an average of sixty six pounds so these heavyweights have hammered 'em unmercifully. The Burners have been batted about, but keep bouncing back, bruises and all, with a fierce determination that's shocking at times. Say Gabe! Those guys trotting out of the locker room—are **all** of them Burner rookies?

Third quarter: Burner rookies went for a field goal. Their fans groaned as the ball was falling way short—but—**suddenly**, the wind got under it, and sailed it through the uprights—it's **good!** Burners by 3. Rebels responded with a touchdown, but the wind did a crazy shift on 'em and they came away with only 6. Burners were forced into another field goal try, and **again**, they got help from the wind. It's 6 all. Rebels scored a second touchdown—12-6, Rebels. When Burner rookies got help from the wind for another 3, the announcers said, "The reigning rookies can't get in the end zone but they can get help from the wind. Burners have 3 field goals, all by wind changes. The Rebels racked up another six, but they can't **buy** an extra point! That's 3 sixes for the Rebels—Rebels 18, Burners 9. Burners are flickering; they need help."

Fourth quarter: Another Burner field goal try—another 3 from the wind. Now **fans** notice the wind's taking sides. It's 18-12, Rebels. The rookies are slow getting up, slow to the huddle, obviously out of steam, but hold 'til the 2 minute warning. They're bushed, but they're not beaten—not yet. During the break, owner, coaches and quarterback form their own huddle. An assistant coach nods toward the bench, and suddenly, players there, who had gone unnoticed, leaped to their feet, ran to the officials and checked in. A murmur rumbled through the crowd. Rebels were on their feet—buzzing like bees. "Are these substitutions legal? Who's this coach that's taken over? **Don't** tell me it's a **woman**! **That** can't be legal! In **our** International League? What's **happened** to football?" They were on fire—yelling and stomping: "This is no place for a woman—ridiculous! Illegal!"

Gabe: "What about it, Mike? Is it legal?"

Mike: "Well, yeah, it's in the rule book, Gabe, but nobody's actually **done** it before—and this has the Rebels **really** upset. They'd better keep their head in the game. This little Jewse ("Juice") College guy has kept these scrappers in the ballgame, Gabe. Let's check in with Lydia down on the field. Lydia, what's going on? Got anything for us up here?

Lydia: Mike and Gabe, the Rebels didn't know it, but this woman, whose name is Sophia, was hired on at the beginning of the season. She chose to stay in the background until this crisis. They **do** listen when she talks—she knows and loves the game—and—she's the **owner's** wife! But there's more to the story—one of the **players** is a woman. That's what really has the Rebels fuming. I'll try to be professional and not say what this woman reporter thinks about their stinking attitude! I'll find out more, Mike."

Gabriel: "It's an end-around. Say! **That** guy runs like John did—and that play clicked like clockwork. Mike, who **are** these fresh players that are running my memory like last season's champs? Did they change quarterbacks?"

Mike: "No, 'Twig' Branch is still in. He's the little guy who got 'em here, Gabe, and Coach is sticking with him. He likes his ball handling—and his sheer guts when the game's on the line. Burner fans are on their feet, cheering wildly for these tired-to-the-bone, underdog rookies, and their 129 pound wonder-boy quarterback! Folks, you may become history makers today!

Gabe: "Injury timeout on the field. The World Champions are re-fired now—**transformed**! These substitutions were a new life-transfusion for 'em, Mike. They went the length of the field these last 3 plays to take the lead, 19 to 18—but the Rebels didn't fold. They ran back the kickoff and took the lead again—wind blew away their extra point again—that has gotten **bizarre**! It stands 24-19. It's been a seesaw ball game. Rebels kicked off and now have the Burners pinned back on their own 3 yard line—less than a minute to play."

Lydia: Mike, Gabe, The woman in the game was recruited by Sophia at the beginning of the season. The ladies are friends of these other players who have come into the game—and get this—they **are** last season champs! No wonder they moved in our memories; they live there. They presented themselves to the league officials, the Burner owner and coaches about the middle of the season, gained eligibility status, and took part in all the closed practice sessions since then. They're playing for love and honor—their only pay! Branded as "scabs," they've played their last game—forever—if the Burners lose. What a story this turned out to be!"

Gabe: "Yeah, and Lydia, what about these women? Wouldn't you say they were, in a way, the key to this whole turnaround? Will that open up the game for women coaches, leaders, and players?"

Mike: Branch is standing back in his own end zone; we can hear him barking signals all the way up here in the booth—is he fired and wired or **what!**"

Gabe: "Yeah, probably thought he'd be pulled when the champs checked in, but the champs watched him play hard—and play hurt most of the season. They want **him** to walk away with a win. The whole team has taken on an in-your-face confidence that just wasn't there before the champions checked in. We still don't have the names of all these players. All right, this could be the last play of the game. Elisha gets down over the ball—the whole team is packed dynamite, begging to blow. "Twig"—heart pounding, mind clicking like a computer, eyes sweeping the field, gets under center: '**Hut, two, three!**' Where did the ball go? That guy **is** lightning! Somebody's fading back—must have the ball. Who **is** he?"

Lydia: David Gaius! Last year's QB—just checked in.

Mike: Gaius will run it—no! He scrambles to his right. He's trapped. **No!** He's free. How'd he get out of **that**? Running to his left, looking downfield. The clock's run out! This is it, folks. Gaius scrambles, buys time, still looking downfield—unbelievable! Who's the Burner in the end zone?

Lydia: Paul Damascus, Gaius's all time favorite long-ball receiver!

Gabriel: Yes! Paul Damascus is waving both hands: "Just **throw** it—I'll get it!" Right-handed Gaius, in his first play of the game is penned in, running left along the one yard line. He can't **possibly** get the ball to Paul—no way—forget it!"

Lydia: But Gaius learned to depend on the wind. On his last step in-bounds, with Rebels on his heels, he cocks his arm and puts the ball in the wind. Who's that on Paul? Thorne, with 6 interceptions for the Rebels! Fans are in a frenzy! Thorne sees it coming—knows he's got number 7. Paul makes a move, fakes Thorne out—as the ball burns past his jaw to hit Damascus smack on the numbers! He cradles it and drops to his knees. **Folks, this ball game is over!** Fans are pouring onto the playing field, goal posts are coming down! Some are carrying players, coaches, Sophia on their shoulders. They're all sweaty, bloody, and muddy—but who cares! Tears look out of place in all the joy and laughter; champagne is forgotten—'til it shows up. Players give it to the coaches; coaches give it to the fans—fans won't drink it. They're pouring it all over each other. One won't drink until they all can—talk about comradary!

Gabe: Un-n-n-n—believable! These rookie lightweights fought with everything they had. When they didn't even have fumes left in their tank, the old vets stepped in like big brothers—just couldn't stand by and watch the game go down! The last season champs put their lives on the line—careers, retirement, everything—for the owner's love, his team, his dream. When the game looked gone, **they** made the difference. Today goes into history as **that day** when it all came together to rout the Rebels.

Michael: Long live Lords' Dynasty! May the Rookies and the Vets—now one—rule for all of you hearing, reading, and longing to share in this dynasty created today when the Burners took out the Rebels. Join all who say, **"This game will never— ever—be the same again."** I have with me, here in the booth, one of the old champs from last season who wrote a lot of the plays used in today's game. First, Jeremiah, would you share with us a little of the background for The Playoff and break down some of the plays you ran and wrote?

Jeremiah: (See Jeremiah 51 NRSV) Well, the Owner family—LORD, God, and Almighty—were very "hands-on" in the early days, and they really worked out the plays. I've kept a record. By the way,

I guess everyone knows the Rebel team is Satan franchised, and Babylon-based. I'll read the notes like I took 'em down from the LORD family:

"1   Thus says the LORD: I am going to stir up **a destructive wind against Babylon**,

2   and I will send winnowers (fanners) to Babylon, and they shall winnow her.

3   **Do not spare** her young men; **utterly destroy her entire army**.

5   Israel and Judah have **not** been forsaken by their God, the LORD of hosts,

    though their land **is** full of guilt before the Holy One of Israel.

6   Flee from the midst of Babylon, save your lives, **each of you**! Do not perish because of **her** guilt, for this is the time of the LORD'S vengeance; he is repaying her what is due.

7   Babylon was a golden cup in the LORD'S hand, making all the earth drunken;

    the nations drank of her wine, and so **the nations went mad**.

8   **Suddenly** Babylon has fallen and is shattered; wail for her!

    Bring balm for her wound; perhaps she may be healed.

9   **We tried** to heal Babylon, but she could not be healed.

    Forsake her, and let each of us go to our own country;

    for her judgment has reached up to heaven and **has been lifted up** even to the skies.

10 The LORD has brought forth our vindication; come, **let us declare in Zion** the work of the LORD our God.

11 Sharpen the arrows! Fill the quivers! The LORD has stirred up the spirit of the kings . . . because his purpose concerning Babylon is to **destroy it**, for that is the vengeance of the LORD, vengeance for his temple.

12 Raise a standard against the walls of Babylon; make the watch strong; post sentinels;

prepare the ambushes; for the LORD has **both planned and done what he spoke** concerning the inhabitants of Babylon. 13You who live by mighty waters, rich in treasures, your end has come, **the thread of your life is cut.**

14 The LORD of hosts has sworn by himself: Surely I will fill you with troops like a **swarm of locusts,** and they shall raise a shout of victory over you.

16 He makes lightnings for the rain, and **he brings out the wind from his storehouses**.

17 Everyone is stupid and without knowledge **(land of the Stupor Bowl)**; goldsmiths are all put to shame by their idols; for their images are false, and there is no breath (wind) in them.

18 They are worthless, a work of delusion; at the

time of their punishment they shall perish. ¹⁹ Not like these is the LORD, **the portion of Jacob,** for he is the one who formed all things, and **Israel is the tribe of his inheritance**; the LORD of hosts is his name.

Israel the Creator's Instrument

²⁰ **You are my war club, my weapon of battle**:
　　with you I smash nations;
　　with you I destroy kingdoms;
²¹ **with you** I smash the horse and its rider;
　　with you I smash the chariot and the charioteer;
²² **with you** I smash man and woman;
　　with you I smash the old man and the boy;
　　with you I smash the young man and the girl;
²³ **with you** I smash shepherds and their flocks;
　　with you I smash farmers and their teams;
　　with you I smash governors and deputies.

(**Now** tell me **who** it is God plans to use to smash the old kingdom and bring in the new?)

The Doom of Babylon

²⁴ I will repay Babylon and all the inhabitants of Chaldea (Babylon) before your very eyes **for all the wrong that they have done in Zion**, says the LORD.
²⁵ I am against you, O destroying mountain,

says the LORD, that destroys the whole earth; **I will stretch out my hand against you, and roll you down from the crags,** and make you a burned-out mountain.

26 No stone shall be taken from you for a corner and no stone for a foundation, but you shall be a perpetual waste, says the LORD.

27 Raise a standard in the land, blow the trumpet among the nations; prepare the nations for war against her, summon against her the kingdoms. . . . appoint a marshal against her, bring up horses like bristling locusts.

28 Prepare the nations for war against her. . . . with their governors and deputies, and every land under their dominion.

29 **The land trembles and writhes**, for the LORD'S purposes against Babylon stand, to make the land of Babylon a desolation, without inhabitant.

30 The warriors of Babylon have given up fighting, they remain in their strongholds; their strength has failed, they have become women; **her buildings are set on fire,** her **bars** are broken.

31 One runner runs to meet another, and one messenger to meet another, to tell the king of Babylon that his city is taken **from end to end**: 32the fords have been seized, the marshes have been

burned with fire, and the soldiers are in panic.

33 For thus says the LORD of hosts, the God of Israel: Daughter Babylon is like a threshing floor at the time when it is trodden; yet a little while and the time of her harvest will come.

34 "King Nebuchadrezzar of Babylon has devoured me, he has crushed me; he has made me an empty vessel, he has swallowed me **like a monster**; he has filled his belly with my delicacies, **he has spewed me out**.

35 May my **torn flesh** be avenged on Babylon," the **inhabitants of Zion shall say.** "May my **blood** be avenged on the inhabitants of Chaldea," **Jerusalem shall say.**

36 Therefore thus says the LORD: I am going to defend your cause and take vengeance for you. I will dry up her sea and make her fountain dry;

37 and Babylon shall become a heap of ruins, a den of jackals, an object of horror and of hissing, without inhabitant.

39 When they are **inflamed**, I will set out their drink and make them drunk, until they become merry and then sleep a perpetual sleep and never wake, says the LORD.

40 I will bring them down like lambs to the slaughter, like rams and goats.

⁴¹ How Sheshach is taken, **the pride of the whole earth seized**!

How Babylon has become an object of horror among the nations!

⁴² **The sea** has risen over Babylon; she has been covered by its tumultuous waves.

⁴³ Her cities have become an object of horror, a land of drought and a desert,

a land in which no one lives, and through which no mortal passes.

⁴⁴ I will punish Bel in Babylon, and **make him disgorge what he has swallowed**.

The nations shall no longer stream to him; the wall of Babylon has fallen.

⁴⁵ **Come out of her, my people! Save your lives, each of you**, from the fierce anger of the LORD!

⁴⁶ Do not be fainthearted or fearful at the rumors heard in the land—one year one rumor comes, the next year another, rumors of violence in the land and of ruler against ruler.

⁴⁷ Assuredly, the days are coming when I will punish the images of Babylon; her whole land shall be put to shame, and all her slain shall fall in her midst.

⁴⁸ **Then the heavens and the earth, and all that is in them, shall shout for joy** over Babylon; for the destroyers shall come against them out of the north. . . .

⁴⁹ Babylon must fall **for the slain of Israel**, as the slain of all the earth have fallen

because of Babylon.

50 You survivors of the sword, go, do not linger! Remember the LORD in a distant land, and **let Jerusalem come into** your mind:

52 Therefore the time is surely coming, says the LORD, when I will punish her idols, and **through all her land the wounded shall groan**.

53 Though Babylon should mount up to heaven, and though she should fortify her strong height, from me destroyers would come upon her, says the LORD.

54 Listen!—a cry from Babylon! A **great crashing** from the land of the Chaldeans!

55 For **the LORD is laying Babylon waste**, and stilling her loud clamor. Their waves roar like mighty waters, the sound of their clamor resounds;

56 for a destroyer has come against her, against Babylon; her warriors are taken, their bows are broken; for the LORD is a God of recompense, he will repay in full.

57 I will make her officials and her sages drunk, also her governors, her deputies, and her warriors; they shall sleep a perpetual sleep and **never wake**, says the King. . . .

58 Thus says the LORD of hosts: The broad

wall of Babylon shall be leveled to the ground, and her high gates shall be **burned with fire**. (The Burners won 'The Playoff!' **Yea for LORD!**') The peoples exhaust themselves for **nothing**, and the nations weary themselves **only for fire**. (The Burners' Lord Dynasty's passion blazes forever.)

61 And Jeremiah said to Seraiah: "When you come to Babylon, see that you read all these words, 62 and say, 'O LORD, you yourself threatened to destroy this place so that neither human beings nor animals shall live in it, and it shall be desolate **forever**.' 63When you finish reading this scroll, **tie a stone to it, and throw it into the middle of the Euphrates,** 64and say, **'Thus shall Babylon sink, to rise no more. . . .'"**

So says The Play-book for The Final Playoff—written—received—done—finished.

CHAPTER 30

The Wild-Child Tree

(Read Romans, Chapters 9, 10, 11)

She's a free-born child, birthed by the Wind—
God made a people where none had been
She's a wild-child, like a flower in the spring—
A wide-eyed wonder-mint kept by the King
The wild-child flower born by the Wind—Grew
up to be a tree where none had been
Whoever heard of any such thing—That from a
wild-child tree one could bring
Fresh holy oil for the grafting on in—Of The
Branch where The Branch has already been?
So wild child could have a ready-trained
mother—To bring her on home, train her and love
her
And make her wild-child olive tree—Be the
Branch of Life for the world to see
Wild-child **does** blossom; her fruit grows—Her

olives are pressed; holy oil flows

Husbandman-King is the One who knows—
How he wants to use the oil that flows

She, considered wild from being born free—
Yields love-olives for the cultivated tree

Wild-child of the nations giving hope to the
Jews—Making new humanity for the King to use

To make the desert bloom and Jerusalem shine—
With oil being crushed from the olive tree-vine

God pleads with **today's** olives:

Love-child olives, born straight out of Me—Will
you be crushed for My family tree?

Love child of mine, born by the Wind—Will you
be crushed to bring Eden again?

Will you worship in my love press—Till your oil
of Life flows holiness?

Will you praise and pray in dedication—For the
King of the Jews to rule his nation?

For the peace of Jerusalem, will you stay—A
living sacrifice, worshipping away

In the crushing of love and regeneration—Till
King David rules his family-nation,

And radiates out to all creation—The Spirit of
Life's love fascination?

Today's olives at FOTB answer:

The fragrance of worship is sniffed by the
Wind—Heaven's final fiddler puts fiddle to chin

He lifts a mighty arm; strings and bow now
merge—Bridal love plays Babylon's funeral dirge

IHOP worshippers breathe Fragrance so sweet—
To grind David's enemies under dancing feet

Praisers and harpers, love-melted into one—

Impart throne-love out through the Son

Sing-praying, Abba Father, your kingdom come—In earth, like heaven, let your heart be done.

Warring worship washes religion all away—Father is glorified through first Adam clay

Last Adam-Yeshua draws in through his side—And Breathes into Father his Blood-bought bride

For Abba to get back his Hebrew Wife—Israel, who fled and bled now gets new Life

Yes! I yield to the crushing, the pressing—The tender love of Abba's caressing

Your wild-child has come home free—Living grafted into You for the world to see

Be it done through me just as you say—Kingdom come this oneness way!

Holy love-crushed oil drips down—To anoint the Root under Blood-soaked ground

Where once more Abba puts Life into clay—Where Messiah cried, "Forgive! Let my Blood stay

To get Abraham and all our kin—A nation and a king to gather us again

The family of God, all one in The Name—From the dust of all the nations, Jews arose and came

Papa ran weeping, open hearted, wide armed—"Come my children where you can't be harmed

The garden of My Heart is blooming again—Eden's fragrance drew you on holy Wind

I inhale your worship, Breathe you up into Me—Then 'shalom you' into Jerusalem made free

Abba talks on:

"We created you in our image, male and female—We inhale you in Yeshua back through the

271

veil

Back into the beginning for Eden again—So is every one who is born by the Wind

Born to be Breathed in and Breathed out again— By My Breath to be carried on my Wind

Till I get my friend Abraham's seed all gathered—From everywhere they've ever been scattered

Till a remnant is a nation that's a living tree— Flowing golden oil, love and Life out of Me."

Church-Israel: Yeshua-Abba, Jesus-Papa, it's done—YeShAbba, we're all pressed into one

God: So you, wild-child olive tree—Through Yeshua became one with Me

Breathing my love to Breathe Israel back in— "Adam" and "Eve," Eden oneness again!

CHAPTER 31

Hearing the God of Abraham, Isaac, and Israel

(**Author's note:** I witnessed this God-encounter. The violent shaking lasted two hours. I knew it hurt—my crying soul told me so. Ann was not functional when the meeting room had to be cleared so she was carried to her friend's car. There, she shook so hard on the back seat that a passerby at the gas station thought she was having a seizure and wanted to call 9-1-1. She had to be carried into her apartment at home hours later. She needed much encouragement to write this and share it—it was so sweet-sensitive to her. **Thanks, Ann**—for sharing, for letting me share it here. We're all blessed by it, and join in your passion for the salvation of Israel and the Jews—and for the end-time, globe-wide harvest. **Shalom Jerusalem**!)

Please understand my purpose for writing this and sharing this most precious experience. I'm not thinking in a theological way when I choose my words, and I don't wish to offend anyone. I'm making a sincere attempt to describe an in-depth experience of the **everlasting** Life of God, using words that I find totally inadequate for the purpose. You may think, "Well, it's not theologically correct for her to **feel** that or to feel **like** that," but I am not judging the experience by theology; I'm just sharing it with you in love.

It happened at The Smithton Revival Network Conference at Lake of the Ozarks, Missouri, July 5, 1999. My pastor, Steve Gray, was preaching about Israel and her importance in coming together with the church in the last great move of God. I began to shake with a Spirit of intercession for this spoken Word to be fulfilled. When the altar call was given, I moved to the sidelines and kept interceding—crying out for God to put the message of destiny for the bride and the Jewish people into the people receiving prayer. As I was praying, the intercession and shaking increased to such a violent shaking that I was taken to my knees, then down on the floor. My body convulsed intensely, far beyond anything I could self-induce. Slowly, everything around me began to fade away. My mind was on the Jewish people and interceding to bring revival into the earth that would make the Jews jealous and draw them into this great move. Then, the earth would see the power of Jesus released again, and true evangelism could really explode.

I can't explain the attitude of desperation that gripped my heart. It was like God and I became one person, meshed together. Then softly, my King and Lord began to expose his heart to me. Never have I **ever** felt such a precious closeness and devotion as when I began to feel the feelings of love that my Father has towards his people! He doesn't get side-tracked or distracted from his purpose for his people—he is very single minded. It was as if he did not care at all for what was going on around me— people praying, talking, leaving. All he cared about at that time with me was the Jewish people being restored and the world being able to receive him through this fulfillment of prophecy. It was like he had been working toward this goal for thousands of years—since Abraham first answered his call, and he first created the Jewish people as a nation. He created a people to represent him in the earth, a people of priests, set apart to accomplish his work and bring him glory, but more than that—the Jews were a people created to be indwelled with the **Person** of God so that God could have a dwelling place here through an intimate connection with his people. This people belonged to God. He deserves to have them, and his heart was so grieved for them!

The intense, violent shaking of intercession continued as waves of the Spirit came over me. I literally lost consciousness as God took me through phases of intercession. Each phase was like a different side of God's heart. There was **so much** emotion! More than a human being could experience on their own apart from God. The intense love and kindness was very deep. It wasn't as if God was **telling** me his feelings; it was more like God was **sharing** his feelings. I felt what he feels—**he put me inside of him and everything he is consumed me**—his goodness and especially his holiness. He was so holy, and I knew that I definitely had nothing righteous in myself that made me worthy to stand in his Presence. But I wanted him so badly, and he was so real and holy that I couldn't speak or bring myself to move out of his Presence. (When God comes that close, you don't move!) He is a King and whatever he wanted, I was going to give him. It wasn't fear alone that motivated me; it was love and a holy, reverent desire to experience the sweetness and intense desperation of **his** love! I wanted to do whatever I had to do to give him what he wanted. God is desperately in love, and jealous, but not in an unjust, negative way. It was kind, firm love. The passion and the jealousy is only for God's people that belong to him to return to him as his possession.

Still shaking violently, I began to feel what the Jews must feel towards the people that were responsible for The Holocaust. To have those things done to your family, ancestors and nation? Imagine the hurt, bitterness, mistrust and pain this opens the door to and lets flood through you. This is just one thing among so many that the Jewish people are forced to deal with now. When a person from the very group of people responsible for The Holocaust comes to minister to the Jews, the Jews have to face all of these walls, even if they are trying to receive ministry. What a hard thing! My heart was flooded with mercy as I cried out to God to help them, heal them, and tear down the walls that the enemy has created in their lives by taking advantage of their pain.

Next, I began to feel an urgent fear of what lies ahead for the nation of Israel. God's Word tells us they will become completely surrounded with armies, and all the nations of the world will turn against them. In their present condition, they will be annihilated. God's love was screaming out for them to become grafted into the vine to prepare them for what's coming. Without God, they don't have a hope. I begged God to draw them to him as the true vine and turn their hearts to believe so they, as a nation, can become grafted into him.

When it seemed God and I had prayed through that phase, his heart turned to Abraham and David and how they feel because of their descendants not being saved—a father's heart breaking for his children! Parents experience such an incredible unselfish love for their children. Without even a second thought, a true father will die to protect his children. I was allowed a glimpse, an emotional "taste" of Abraham and David's hearts as they broke down in desperation for their children to be restored to them. We, as Christians, fight and believe for our families to belong to God and to walk in the covenants of God. We expect that blessing to rest upon our children, their children and their children. Our hearts are crushed with unbearable grief when our descendants are snatched out of the hand of God, and an enemy defiles them and locks them in a prison of torment. This very thing happened to Abraham and David's descendants. Their hearts are torn for their children to return into the fold. Damnation, condemnation, and destruction oppress the very people that were given the covenants of God and the kingdom of God. They are the ones that should be carrying the power and glory of God into the earth to the world. Evangelism belongs to the Jews. The Jewish people deserve to experience this wonderful glory that we are experiencing. In the Old Testament, when the Israelites got in trouble, they cried out to God and he remembered his covenant with Abraham, Isaac and Jacob, and he would come to their rescue. I wondered if he would do the same thing **today—if we cry out on their behalf.** I was going to try it—going to find out. If it worked for them then, it will work for us now.

Then, my heart was pierced through as God revealed one last thing. Because so few of the Jewish people know Jesus as their Messiah, and don't belong to him, death is in their lives. They don't belong to the kingdom of light. Death's darkness, somehow, intertwines their souls, bodies, minds, hearts, families, finances and more. When God fought for the Israelites back in Egypt, when they were slaves to the Egyptians, the Egyptians experienced the curses and plagues, not the Israelites! All through the Bible, the pagans had death, sickness, destruction and torment, but the people of God were protected by God. The death angel came to the Egyptians, not the Jews. But now, death has made its way into Israel—where it does not belong. When that revelation came to me, it was the straw that broke the camel's back. My heart broke for my Father. I yielded myself to the Spirit of intercession, even though by this time it was painful because I had been shaking so strong for so long. I thought, if this could somehow help my God save his people, I'm willing. That must have been the attitude Jesus had about the pain when they put the nails in his hands.

To describe what the sweet Presence of God felt like during this time seems impossible. It is so difficult, and my best efforts and words fall so far short that I came very close to not even trying. My thought was just to leave off this part, because after I wrote it, it fell so very, very short of expressing the essence of the experience. Yet, the purpose for which I entered into the experience cries out in me to go ahead and do the best I can and pray God smiles on my efforts.

I could feel waves of glory like a wind of kindness **flow** over me. Every time it would **flow** over me, I would go back into unconsciousness. It wasn't the kind of wind that blows **over**; it was more like it went **through** me, **consuming** every fiber of my being. Everything around me would fade and God's brightness would increase. It was very bright with him and clear. His thoughts were clear but not in words—more like waves of emotion, but not the kind of emotion that leaves you feeling torn and upset. It was emotion saturated in love and peace that was somehow **absorbed into me**. I must have said this to myself a hundred times: "I have to get up; I have to go home." Within seconds of the thought, I would drift back to God and the Jewish people.

Here's a part that is **really** impossible to communicate. I am trying to use words for something that did not come to me in words. It came by way of this incredible everlasting **impartation** of God! I am still working through the understanding of the experience myself, but if I wait until I fully understand it before sharing it—well, that could be a long, long time! Again, I don't mean to offend, and I'm not out to change theology, or start any doctrines, or correct any. I'm simply sharing an **experience**, all right? In this experience, God revealed Himself to me and imparted to me—communicating with me **as if he, Himself, were a Jew**. The impartation—the love, the feelings, the revelations, the whole experience left me with this: **God is a Jew. That is who he is, and I felt that, as I was connecting with the Jews, I was connecting with him.**

I felt very light but very heavy at the same time. I felt like I was floating, but my body wouldn't move; it was glued to the floor. The awe of God in his holiness was so incredible that I was almost afraid to move. He is so holy and pure and I didn't want to go back to a defiled world. I knew that with him was life. He could hear and answer. **I knew he could save the Jewish people and I was so close to him, I**

knew he heard me. I didn't want to leave because I didn't want to quit praying until I got a breakthrough for Israel. I knew as long as I stayed with him, I would be safe. God is a Person, and to be with him was more than strange feelings. It was to see who he is—his character. He is powerful, yet kind; loving, yet holy; pure goodness, without any trace of compromise or unrighteousness. I had never seen that kind of holiness and righteousness. He was so holy that I almost felt as if I shouldn't talk or move because I might dishonor him, and he would go away, and I didn't want him to leave. Everything else in my life completely faded into irrelevancy. He was all that mattered. There are times in my life when I get convicted and am concerned with what will happen when I die. What will God say when I stand before the judgment seat? Will I be a goat and God will have to say, "Depart from me, you evil doer?" But while this experience was taking place, I felt so close to God that any of that kind of thinking would have been totally inappropriate. I didn't want to think of any of that, and I didn't want to leave because I knew at this moment in his Presence, I was received and accepted.

The experience itself left me with a new sensitivity in my heart to God and the Jews. It did something inside of me, **like my Father left a trace of Himself with me**—as if I had been **branded** with a new vision of urgency and soberness of the heart of God. There is inside of me a new merciful patience. I want to go back to that place in the Spirit with God and be with him again like that. Only, this time I want to stay with him longer to see what he will do.

To even think about trying to measure the experience by my present state of understanding would tend toward forcing the experience to fit into the confines of my mind as it is now and throw me toward "judging" which part was God and which was not. That causes me to shudder. **No! No! No! It was all God**, don't you see? **Therefore, I must seek him out and let my understanding of him change and grow.** That's my approach in seeking to understand this experience with my everlasting Father. These scriptures now have new meaning to me:

Amos 9

⁹ "For surely I will command, And will sift the house of Israel among all nations, As grain is sifted in a sieve; **Yet not the smallest grain shall fall to the ground**.

¹¹ **"On that day I will raise up The tabernacle of David**, which has fallen down, And repair its damages; I will raise up its ruins, And rebuild it as in the days of old;

¹² **That they may possess** the remnant of Edom, And **all the Gentiles who are called by My name,"** Says the LORD who does this thing.

¹⁴ I will bring back the captives of My people Israel; They shall build the waste cities and inhabit them;

¹⁵ **I will plant them in their land, And no longer shall they be pulled up from the land I have given them,"** Says the LORD your God.

Psalm 122

"2 Our feet have been standing within your gates, O Jerusalem!.

5 For thrones are set **there** for judgment, the thrones of the house of David.

6 Pray for the peace of Jerusalem: "May they prosper who love you.

7 Peace be within your walls, Prosperity within your palaces."

8 For the sake of my brethren and companions, I will now say, "Peace be within you."

Zechariah

12:3 "And it shall happen in that day that I will make Jerusalem a very heavy stone for all peoples; **all who would heave it away will surely be cut in pieces**, though all nations of the earth are gathered against it.

4"In that day," says the LORD, **I will open My eyes on the house of Judah. . . .**

6 "In that day I will make the governors of Judah like a firepan in the woodpile, and like a fiery torch in the sheaves; **they shall devour all the surrounding peoples** on the right hand and on the left, but **Jerusalem shall be inhabited again in her own place. . . .**

8 "In that day the LORD will defend the inhabitants of Jerusalem; the one who is feeble among them in that day shall be like David, and **the house of David shall be like God**, like the angel of the Lord before them.

9 "It shall be in that day that I will seek to

destroy all the nations that come against Jerusalem.

[10] "And I will pour on the house of David and on the inhabitants of Jerusalem the Spirit of grace and supplication; then they will look on Me whom they pierced.

[11] "In that day there shall be a great mourning in Jerusalem. . . .

13:1 **"In that day a fountain shall be opened for the house of David and for the inhabitants of Jerusalem, for sin and for uncleanness.**

[8] And it shall come to pass in all the land," Says the LORD, **"That two-thirds in it shall be cut off and die, But one-third shall be left in it:**

[9] I will bring the one-third through the fire, will refine them as silver is refined, And test them as gold is tested. They will call on My name, And I will answer them. **I will say, 'This is My people'; And each one will say, 'The LORD is my God.'"**

14: [3] Then **the LORD will go forth And fight against those nations.** [4] And in that day His feet will stand **on the Mount of Olives, Which faces Jerusalem on the east.**

[5] **Thus the LORD my God will come, And all the saints with You.**

[8] And in that day it shall be that **living waters shall flow from Jerusalem**, Half of them toward the eastern sea And half of them toward the western sea; In both summer and winter it shall occur.

[9] And the LORD shall be King over all the earth. In that day it shall be; "The LORD is one," And His name one.

[10] Jerusalem shall be raised up and **inhabited in her place**. Jerusalem shall be **safely inhabited**.

1 Kings
"But King Solomon shall be blessed, and **the throne of David shall be established** before the LORD **forever**." (1 Ki 2:45 NKJV)

Isaiah
"For unto us a Child is born, Unto us a Son is given; And the government will be upon His shoulder. And His name will be called Wonderful, Counselor, Mighty God, Everlasting Father, Prince of Peace. Of the increase of His government and peace, there will be **no end, upon the throne of David and over his kingdom,** to order it and establish it with judgment and justice from that time forward, even **forever**." (Isa 9:6, 7 NKJV)

Jeremiah
"Then shall enter the gates of this city kings and princes sitting on **the throne of David. . . and this city shall remain forever."** (Jer 17:24, 25 NKJV)

Luke
"He shall be great, and shall be called the Son of the Highest: and the Lord God shall give unto him **the throne of his father David. . . .** And he shall reign **over the house of Jacob for ever**; and of his kingdom there shall be no end." (Luke 1:32, 33 KJV)

The Revelation

'These things says He who is holy, He who is true, "He who has **the key of David**, He who opens and no one shuts, and shuts and no one opens." (Rev 3:7 NKJV)

"I, Jesus, have sent My angel to testify to you these things in the churches. **I am the Root and the Offspring of David, the Bright and Morning Star."** (Rev 22:16 NKJV)

"What I Wouldn't Give"
Copyright © 2002 Daniel Gray
(Used by permission)

(The LORD Almighty touches the earth and it melts; all who live in it **mourn.** The LORD roars from Zion, **and utters His voice from Jerusalem**; the pastures of the shepherds **mourn. The king will mourn**, the prince will be **clothed with despair**, and the hands of the people of the land will **tremble**. I will pour out on the house of David and the inhabitants of Jerusalem a spirit of grace and supplication. They will look on me, the one they have pierced, and they will **mourn** for him as one mourns for an only child, and **grieve bitterly** for him as one grieves for a firstborn son. On that day the weeping in Jerusalem will be great. The land will **mourn.** The **fishermen** will groan and lament. See Amos 9:5, Amos 1:2 NKJV, Zech 12:10-12, Ez 7:25-27, Isa 19:8 NKJV)

1

Early in the morning as I lie in bed—**I can hear**

that Voice echo in my head

It wasn't too small and it wasn't too still—But it always helped me know my Father's will

I learned about life and I learned about sin—What I wouldn't give to hear that Voice again

2

Living as a Christian has its ups and downs—I've had a lot of good times and a lot of frowns

Times when no one thought I had the knack—When I heard that Voice it got me back on track

Daniel's still surviving in the lion's den—But what I wouldn't give to hear that Voice again

(chorus)

So get louder—say it once again. And be bolder—tell it like it is

And be stronger—say it just a little—Bit longer—we can take some more

What I wouldn't give, what I wouldn't give, what I wouldn't give to hear that Voice again

3

Seen a lot of trouble paying up my dues—Christians hate each other and they hate the Jews

Churches full of apathy and full of doubt—There's only one Voice that can straighten 'em all out

Don't know what to make of the times we're in—What I wouldn't give to hear that Voice again.

Because We Hear, She'll Hear (See Isaiah 66):

7   "Before she goes into labor, she gives birth;
before the pains come upon her, she
delivers a son. 8Who has ever heard
of such a thing? Who has ever seen
such things? Can a country be born in
a day or a nation be brought forth in a
moment?

**Yet no sooner is Zion in labor than she
gives birth to her children.**

9   **"Do I bring to the moment of birth and not
give delivery?" says the LORD.**

**"Do I close up the womb when I bring to
delivery?"** says your God.

10   "Rejoice with Jerusalem and be glad for her,
all you who love her; rejoice greatly
with her, all you who mourn over her.

11   **For you will nurse and be satisfied at her
comforting breasts;**

you will drink deeply and delight in her
overflowing abundance."

"I will extend peace to her like a river, and
the wealth of nations like a flooding
stream;

you will nurse and be carried on her arm and
dandled on her knees.

13   As a mother comforts her child, so will I
comfort you; and you will be
comforted over Jerusalem." 15See,
**the LORD is coming with fire, and
his chariots are like a whirlwind;** he
will bring down his anger with fury,

and his rebuke with **flames of fire**.
16 **For with fire and with his sword** the LORD
will execute judgment upon all men,
and many will be those slain by the LORD.
18 "And I, because of their actions and their
imaginations, am about to come and
gather all nations and tongues, and
they will come and see my glory.
19"I will set a sign among them, and **I
will send some of those who survive
to the nations**. They will proclaim
my glory among the nations. 20And
they will bring all your brothers, from
all the nations, to my holy mountain
in Jerusalem as an offering to the
LORD. 22"As **the new heavens and
the new earth that I make will
endure before me**," declares the
LORD, "**so will your name and
descendants endure**."

(See also Revelation 21.)

CHAPTER 32

Let Jerusalem Come Into Your Mind

———————>•○•<———————

Jeremiah 51 (NRSV)

5 **"Israel and Judah have not been forsaken**
by their God, the LORD of hosts,
though their land is full of guilt before the
Holy One of Israel. [10]The LORD has
brought forth our vindication; come,
let us declare **in Zion** the work of the
LORD our God.

19 Not like these is the LORD, the portion of
Jacob, for he is the one who formed
all things, and **Israel is the tribe of
his inheritance;** the LORD of hosts
is his name.

Israel the Creator's Instrument

20 "**You are my war club, my weapon of battle:**
with you I smash nations; **with you I destroy** kingdoms;**
21 **with you I smash** the horse and its rider; **with you I smash** the chariot and the charioteer;
22 **with you I smash** man and woman; **with you I smash** the old man and the boy;
with you I smash the young man and the girl;
23 **with you I smash** shepherds and their flocks; **with you I smash** farmers and their teams; **with you I smash** governors and deputies. [35]'**May my torn flesh be avenged. . . ,'** the inhabitants of Zion shall say. '**May my blood be avenged. . . ,'** Jerusalem shall say.
50 You survivors of the sword, go, do not linger! **Remember the LORD in a distant land, and <u>let Jerusalem come into your mind</u>. . . ."**

I'm counting myself included in with these Jews who are asked to let Jerusalem come into their mind. I'm listening to God through another Jew, Zechariah: "[4]On that day his feet (Adonai's) shall stand on the **Mount of Olives**, which lies before Jerusalem on the east; and the Mount of Olives shall be split in two. . . then the LORD my God will come, **and all the holy ones with him**." (Zechariah 14 NRSV)

I'm letting Jerusalem come into my mind, and I'm banking on the Mount of Olives. Opened an account there—The Mountain Trust Bank. When I saw from Zech that Yeshua's favorite landing spot on earth would be there, and he was bringing all his gang with him to hang out there, I said, "Man, how can I go wrong doing business with that bank?" I may be slow—stupid I'm not. Unch-uh. I figure this way: every time I let Jerusalem come into my mind, and do something in that direction, "chungh": there went a spiritual deposit into The Mountain. When I get blessed, I say, "Thank you, Lord God of Abraham, Isaac, Jacob, David, Jesus and all the rest." "Chungh"—spiritual deposit hit. When I pray for the peace of Jerusalem, there it went again— "Chungh." I'm banking on the mountain.

Why does lightning land out of heaven where it does? I always thought it just flashed out of heaven and "kapow!" hit the ground at random. Found out, not so. Seems certain conditions in the ground cause an energy buildup, like a force field. Energy in the sky sends lightning zigzagging, craving this big energy bank in earth that's begging a strike!"

Here's how I've got it figured: if enough of us open accounts in The Mountain Trust Bank where Yeshua's got his big lifetime savings stashed, we'll create **such** an upward-power-surge-eruption that he'll just have to zap on down and strike feet-first right there on The Mountain Bank.

Think about all the churches in the world letting

Jerusalem come into their minds, directing their individual and corporate spiritual wealth to build up the force field. The pulling-down-from-heaven force field in The Mountain reaches a cannot-be-denied level. Wow! Then that consuming-fire God **couldn't wait** to strike on down. Thing is, I don't know how many are doing that, do you?

If every activity of every person in every church, no matter what they were doing—praying, healing, casting out demons, bringing people to God, loving, protecting, nurturing, everything—if they would **let Jerusalem come into their mind** as part of the **purpose** for it, there would be such electric-like waves hitting The Mountain that the energy-impulse factor would kick in. Father's heart, Super sensitive to all such activity, would joyfully jump right down on The Mountain with us. Man! What a **plan**! God, you're the **greatest** I know.

Does Jerusalem come into your mind too? Like it does mine? Bet it does. Let's spread the word. **Shalom Jerusalem!** Jews, we're your co-depositors in earth. We're pulling on God's heart with you. Kingdom, **come!** Churches, **deposit**. Christians, **deposit**. Minds, **let Jerusalem come in**. Israel, **be birthed**. Father's will, **be done**—in **earth**, on the Mount of Olives, east in Zion, **just like** it is in heaven. **Come**, Messiah Yeshua, **come**; come **quickly**. We **love** you. Amen. I'm encouraged. A twig or two of non-Jewish Christians are getting truly grafted in.

CHAPTER 33

I Need to Bring Them

———⟫•◦•⟪———

"Yes, indeed! I tell you, the person who doesn't enter the sheep-pen through the door, but climbs in some other way, is a thief and a robber. But the one who goes in through the gate is the sheep's own shepherd. This is the one the gate-keeper admits. **I am the gate** for the sheep. All those who have come before me have been thieves and robbers. **I am the gate**; if someone enters through me, he will be safe and will go in and out and find pasture. I lay down my life on behalf of the sheep. Also I have other sheep which are not from this pen; **I need to bring them,** and there will be **one flock, one shepherd**. This is why the Father loves me; because I lay down my life—in order to take it up again." (See John 10:1-17 CJB.)

Yeshua is talking to Jews: "I need to bring them." He needs to do what? "**Bring** them." Bring who? Bring me and you—the non Jew. He's telling the Jews to make room for the non Jews to get in the door—make room in their thinking, their lives, their **nation**, their kingdom, for the Gentiles. "Get out of your 'we have an exclusive franchise on the God of Abraham, Isaac, and Israel' mindset. Quit blocking the door against the Gentiles and let the nations come on into the nation of Israel and share the glory and the kingdom of God in Israel."

I want to leave with you the picture God stamped into me. Imagine God's Life is the "filling" within the whole, big picture "frame." God has covered and **embraced** a little nation. This little nation, Israel, is **encased** in this great big God, and is called his wife. This wife birthed God a Son named Yeshua. This Son, Yeshua, is **encased** inside Israel. There's Abba embracing and encasing Israel—Israel embracing and encasing Yeshua. Here is Yeshua saying, "I am the gate." Now a gate does not just set out in the field all by its lonesome itself. A gate is a portal—an entrance—to something. Its reason for existence is connected with some larger entity. What is the larger entity for which Jesus, the God-Gate exists? Jesus is **not** a lone entity with no attachment. Then, where's he attached? He's always been the God-Gate to Father in the Spirit—but, **in the earth**, the entity for which Yeshua has always been the God-Gate is **Israel** (who is encased in Father's heart). Yeshua is eternally **encased** in Israel, the mother who bore him, and she, in turn is encased in Abba Elohim—in Father God. Abba is the Gatekeeper—Jesus the Gate—Israel the Gate-holder of the Gate for the Gatekeeper.

Here's a shakeup shot of the wakeup I got. It comes in three short snaps: **(1)** Enter through the narrow gate; **small is the gate** and **only a few find it**. (See Matthew 7:13, 14) **(2)** Make every effort to enter through the narrow door, because **many, I tell you, will <u>try to enter</u> and will <u>not</u> be able to**. (See Luke 13:24) Only a **few** find this gate? Many **try to enter** (maybe **think** they've entered?) and won't make it? Now the third part is the torch burning in my gut. **(3)** If I'm **not** looking and hooking with this Jesus who's **encased** forever into **Israel**, with "Messiah **of Israel**" written all over him—with "**King of the Jews**" as his thigh-side tattoo, what "lord" have I been sold by some slickster standing on his polished platform-soapbox? If I didn't enter into the kingdom of God that's Israel-embraced by Abba—where her Messiah is Israel-encased as the Gate to her, her King and kingdom, then what, pray tell, **have** I entered into? If anything? A mirage? A delusion? A brilliant, man-minded, Jew-rejecting, Gentile formation of a **false**, non Jewish "lord" and **his** "church?" Sobering questions, I tell you. "For even if there are so-called gods, whether in heaven or on earth (as **indeed there are many "gods" and many "lords"**),

yet **for us** there is but one God, the Father, from whom all things came and for whom we live; and **there is but one Lord, Jesus Christ (and he's forever tied to Israel!)**, through whom all things came and through whom we live. (See 1 Corinthians 8:5, 6)

This God-Gate Lord is **set in** as **Israel's**

Messiah—he'll **never** be another nation's Messiah. **This** God-Gate Lord's Daddy, "God, the Father" is the Gatekeeper who **did** the **setting in** of Yeshua as Jerusalem, Israel's Gate. He has never—and will never—make him a gate to **any other city or any other nation.** Is **he** the one I have? Then I'm connected to Israel—I mean **today's** Israel—the one down on the dirt-ground that Gatekeeper and God-Gate are working with and working in to rule a worldwide kingdom of love and peace—terror free!

I visualize this working in double dimension: earth-side and heaven-wide. **In earth**, Israel—embracing and encasing Yeshua—"houses" God for his earthly headquarters in Jerusalem. That's God's home base, just like it was for the first David, son of Jesse. Out from there goes the Torah teachings of the Spirit of life throughout Israel, then out to the nations, and all creation. Out from Israel the world will be "harvested." ("Ask of me, and I will make the nations your inheritance, the ends of the earth your possession" was spoken first to the Jews.) The God-Gate is open to **bring** nations into—and Jews **back** into Jerusalem, Israel. "I have other sheep which are not from this pen (here, now in Israel); **I need to bring them**," Jesus said.

Here's how I visualize it in earth now. Yeshua is standing as a "hole-in-the-wall" of Jerusalem (encased in Israel, which is encased in Father). The gate—the door, the portal—is in the shape of Yeshua's earthly body but it's now **glorified**, invisible, translucent, warmly drawing and welcoming strangers and friends alike into the city—Jesus, the

ultimate "tour guide."

Jeremiah spoke the word of the Lord to Jews scattered throughout the nations, "Remember the LORD in a distant land, and **let Jerusalem come into your mind**." (Jer 51:50 NRSV) I can let Jerusalem come into **my** mind, as well as the scattered Jews can. When I **do** this, Jerusalem becomes "a state of mind," that leads to "a state (Israel) **in** my mind." In this spiritual working, the "state" of Jerusalem (Israel) forms in my mind and heart, and I am **drawn** by the Holy Spirit in my spirit toward Jerusalem.

Here's the cool part. This Yeshua-Gate is a **living** gate—a **traveling** gate—a portable portal. He has "trans-port-er" capability. He can gather me into himself as the city gate and carry me (like Samson took the city gates to the top of the hill) to the top of the mountain. This is the **heaven-wide** dimension to coincide with the **earth-side**. This is how we can start (this very second) to "enter into Jerusalem," and become a part of Jerusalem, Israel that is now screaming in the agony of labor to give birth to her Husband-Creator's destiny as his wife in earth. We can **help her** (not **replace** her!) in these labor pains by letting Jerusalem come into our mind—by giving her a place in our hearts, our love, our gifts, our prayers, our time, our money.

Your **old** theology (is there a dumpster nearby?) may not allow this, but in Revelations 21, I see Yeshua **encased** and living in the twelve Jew-tribe-gates, in the twelve Jew-apostle-foundations. (Luke became a "Jew at heart" and showed me how to do it.) Jesus is **encased** in all that's there and **embraced** by the whole mother-city which is inside and one with Father, who "frames" it all, fosters and enflames them all with his love.

With the **heaven-wide** dimension, I can come to this Yeshua "Pearly-Gate" that David saw ever before his face, and he'll "gather me in" for "Gate-holding." He reserves the right to hold me in the "Gate" until he decides whether to hook me directly into **earth-side** Jerusalem now, or work on me for **heaven-wide** use—to be hooked up **indirectly** (or "caught up" later and trans-port-ed) **into earth-side** Jerusalem from **heaven-wide Jerusalem**. He can do it lots of ways, **at the same time**, in more than two dimensions and from angles eternity-wide. And, you know **what**? I really don't care about the **how**, and the **when**—but I would really like to take care of the **whether**. I want to make sure that it **does** take place **some** how, **some** "when." With Jesus encased in, and living in, all the gates and all the foundations of the new, **eternal** Jerusalem, I've been given Gatekeeper trust that he will receive me into his Jerusalem God-Gate gathering right now. (**Why risk getting "left behind?"** Just get "hauled up" early! That'll take **care** of **that** kind o' stuff.)

So let's **do** it: "Lord Jesus, right now, I accept by faith that you are alive—been raised up from the dead since dying in my place—and that you, being no respecter of persons, stand alive before me right now—just like you stood before John after the resurrection—clothed on and one with Father by the Spirit. I remember your words, "Blessed are those who have not seen, but believe anyhow." Lord, I believe **anyhow.** I believe you're encased, embraced and living in Father in the gates of the **new** Jerusalem—that as you stand before me, new Jerusalem stretches out behind you, over you, all around you, and below you, and pours out over me right now to swallow me up inside you, inside the city that embraces you and encases you, and on up into and inside our Abba who embraces and encases us all. I receive your Spirit covering me to swallow me up in your Spirit from the bottom of my feet to the top of my head into the city of new Jerusalem. I yield now to your Spirit and receive you swallowing me on up. I say with your faith that lives in me, Jesus Lord, "You **have** done it; it **is** finished. I **am** part of Jerusalem—I am part of Israel, one way or another—or both. Now, **use** me working **earth-side** to pull new Jerusalem down over old Jerusalem to establish your kingdom city in earth. Use me all up 'til you're ready to take me all up **heaven-wide** for that big family reunion—right down, over, through, and out of down-to-the-mountain-dirt-Jerusalem, Israel. It is finished—it **has** been done!" Jesus said, "I need to **bring them.**" Bring us all, Lord. We say, "We need to be brought."

Addendum

Shocked! The word's not strong enough to describe my feeling. It was Friday—manuscript going in the mail **no later than** Monday! Though I didn't see one, she had to be "tied out" there close by—that white mare out of heaven that brought the fiery redhead to **"Blow the Trumpet/Sound the Alarm Conference"** at Christ Triumphant Church (CTC) in Lee's Summit, Missouri. I had never heard the woman, never read the woman—**not a word**; she didn't know **I** existed. **Yet**, she fired up, **and preached this book! What a blessed confirmation.** Bonnie is working to get this message out in a book, but meantime, you could go online at www.christtri-umphant.org and order the tapes from CTC. Ask for **Bonnie Chavda's** "3 Marks of the Spirit in the End Times Church" from the **"Blow the Trumpet/ Sound the Alarm Conference,"** Friday, December 13, 2002, 7:00 PM. If I were you, I'd **order the**

videos and let Bonnie all up in my face with God's fire to cut my head-shackles loose and let my heart run free.)

Also, www.bonniechavda will get you to Mahesh Chavda Ministries Intl. Home Page where you can click on "If We Are Silent" to read and sign a resolution of support for Israel, assuming this is still active when you're reading this. Either way, this is the place to get their ministries and to watch for Bonnie's new book.

Glossary of Terms— What the Words Mean *to Me*

———➤◦◄———

3-thru

A working of God involving three couples: (1) Son-church, (2) Father-Israel, (3) husband-wife. These 3 couples are main players in the process of regenerating new creatures for the new earth age. I see what I term a "3-thru" working of God **by** Holy Spirit, **through** Holy Spirit. As part of this 3-thru, the bride church is gathered into and taken by God **through** Bridegroom Christ **into Israel**, Father's earthly wife (into Father's Israel-based plan). Son and Father are already one God by Holy Spirit. As Son's church-bride becomes one "wife" with Father's nation-wife (Israel), Son and Father become one "husband." Church and Israel become one "wife." At this stage, the two "couples" have become one couple and that couple one entity. That's a "2-thru": Christ and his bride, Abba and his wife have "worked through" to oneness. Abba and his Son are one—Abba's "wife" and Son's "wife" are one with each other and **one with Abba-Son**. You could call this "a 4-in-one," but the working involves 2 couples—Bridegroom and Church, Maker-Husband and Israel.

One more couple is needed for a 3-thru—**and**—a "3-peat." (Just stay with me now—get your money's worth!) So happens, the Master Creator, who knows how to zoom through from Alpha to Omega, also knows how to **plant** Omega back into a **fresh** alpha and **perpetuate** Omega through **that** alpha all the way to a **fresh** omega—and then spin this process into perpetual motion (eternal Spirit). This fresh alpha is the earthly humankind couple, husband and wife. God can now live out through **last** Adam men and women "in his likeness and in his image." God, through this new God-Creature, lives out through men—**married or not**—to reveal his male likeness. God, through this new God-Creature, lives out through **women—married or not**—to reveal his female likeness. (In **Christ** there is not male and female—in **Father** there is **both**. Come on now, you gotta read the whole book where I explain all this.) YeShAbba, himself (with "herself" inside and one-with), wills and loves to put men and women together in his plan for their destinies to be fulfilled. He loves and **flows** them together in and by Holy Spirit—through this God-Creature (Himself).

Then he loves and flows **out through** them in the new earth. A man and woman don't just "marry prayerfully." They're **flowed** together in Abba love by Holy Spirit.

Let's review: the 3-thru working, then, is (1) Son-church, (2) Father-Israel, (3) Husband-wife. Son-church flows into Father-Israel where Son-Father is already one; church-Israel become one, making Father-Son-church-Israel one. **Then**, this is expressed into the (new or becoming new) earth—by a human husband "housing" and becoming one with Father-Son, by a human wife "housing" and becoming one with church-Israel. By this Spirit-merging, husband and wife become one flesh, indwelled by God-Creature, who, **in this stage** of "new heavens and new earth," is really Father, Mother, Son. From such parents, children are born in the new earth as was John the Baptist (filled with the Spirit in the womb) and Yeshua. Father is working all this to answer Jesus' prayer: "Father, I pray that we may all be one."

Babylon (as used in **this** book)

I call Babylon **any** system of belief, built, knowingly **or unknowingly**, on and around **humankind's old-Adam nature**, using, as foundation, thought systems, rudiments, and rhythms that **interfere** with God **personally** holding his family in the Holy Spirit. It's a battle of some system—**any** system—versus **Holy** Spirit; that's the sum-of-it. If it's **not** Spirit, then it's system. If it's not Holy Spirit, it's **unholy** spirit from the anti-Christ spirit horde.

Bottom line: Christ **Holy** Spirit versus **anti**-Christ unholy spirit, with "anti" meaning "against" **or "instead of."** Does God require a system in which to gather his people? No! He does not. There's a fine (but living or dying) line between "organization" and "system." Truth does **not** need a man-thought-up system for the Spirit to work in—the **anti-Christ** spirit **does** need a system. That system, with all its ramifications and octopus-like tentacles, is revealed in Scripture as spiritual Babylon which means "confusion." **There** is where man's **unregenerate** intellect pole-vaulted itself into "Christian" gatherings and offered its wonderful assistance to set up man-contrived systems. God's people were "slickened" out from under the control of the Spirit. The Holy Spirit is well empowered to reveal, impart, implant, **order**, and preserve truth **without any** help from man's pride-soaked intellect. Spirit resurrects the mind of Christ in the body of Christ and **Spirit-orders** what's needed. Spirit has his own order, and reserves exclusive and absolute "copyrights" to **change this order.** Once a system gets rolling, you can't change that sucker—and you can't shift it. Satan's got the gut-gears of it. (You can say "organization" instead of "order" as long as you distinguish "organization" from "system.") Systems are **usually** crystallized, galvanized, fossilized, organized and advertised **Spirit-order of what God was doing yesterday!** The Spirit **moved** on, but the system **stayed** on. It's impossible for us to over-imagine how supernaturally clever the sliding serpent is in this. He usually uses **the same words** of God's yesterday order. That's why the Spirit constantly changes "order" in some way **in order** to block out Satan, the "systemizer," "crystalizer," "galvanizer," organizer and **ultimate** advertiser. Spirit perpetuates the life of God, system perpetuates system—loves **system** itself, for the sake of itself, and hides itself under spiritualized dressings (like being "great guardians and protectors of the faith.")

Because they've **all** become walls of division, **all** must fall—**all walls fall**—all of anti-Christ, instead-of-Christ Babylon—all denominational structures, all shades and flavors of old Adam-man superiority-over-Spirit sheds, religious organizations, **inward-focused** church empires and mega-churches, **inward-focused, personality powered** "ministries"— all cleverly cogged and clogged, full of the "my, my, my"; "mine, mine, mine"; "whine, whine, whine"; "pay, pay, pay"; "give, give, give"; "drive, drive, drive"; "go, go, go get 'ems"—**all** these vehicle systems, large or small, that end up **displacing** the Holy Spirit's control. **God is sick o' the mess!** He has one **vehicle** in which to hold his disciples—the one body of Jesus—called together, put together, and held together by the one Holy Spirit. "Just as **the body is one** and has many members, and **all the members** of the body, though many, **are one body, so it is with Christ**. For **in the one Spirit** we were **all baptized into one body**— and we were **all made to drink of one Spirit**. (See I Cor 12:12-14 NRSV) I'm oversimplifying? Oh well! Go tell. It's long overdue—but, **"Oh, what shall we do?"** cry the Babylon boatloads. Well, why don't we **all** just get outta the boat and **head for God, walking on the water?** If he can't keep us by the Spirit, we're sunk anyhow! Let's quit "going to Egypt" for help—or in this case, bolting to Babylon for backup—just in case we start sinking! If we sink, we sink—reaching and crying out, "Lord, **save us!**"

It's Spirit, **not** system, who "organizes" us in God. Spirit **orders** us properly in God—He's **God's** "Orderer Part"—**Everything else is Babylon**—in **this** book. (Yours I don't know about.) I know **this**—be it oversimplified or whatever: The woman was clothed in purple and scarlet, and adorned with gold and jewels and pearls (**She looks really good, but what is she "holding?"**), holding in her hand a golden cup (Looks good on the outside, but what's it "**holding**?"), full of abominations and the impurities of her fornication; and on her forehead (that **great** human intellect) was written a name, a mystery (**now being revealed**): "**Babylon the great, mother of whores** and (mother) of earth's abominations." **She's in "the church"** and she's **looking** super nifty, smelling spiritually spiffy.) And I saw that the woman was drunk (confused, not using the mind of Christ in the one clear Spirit) with the blood (lives) of the saints and the blood (lives) of the witnesses to Jesus. (See Rev 17:4-6) Drunk on believers' life-blood. She's **using** believers, **not only to support her long-standing mother system, but using believers' lives to spawn other spider web holding nets. She's mother to all the smaller cistern-system holders.**

Pastor Alan Koch said last Sunday—after coming back from the transformed city of Almalonga, Guatemala—"I see this as our big problem: every time God does something, **we try to fit it into the system.**" Bull's eye, pastor! That's why we're still battling babbling Babylon, instead of basking on God's boundless love beaches in his full-blown kingdom. It is Spirit **or** (not "and") system. If you don't draw the line here, "Every system does what's right in its own eyes," and that system **always** eventually becomes **self** perpetuating. System is **not** going to fit into Spirit. **Spirit is not going to compromise to fit** into **any** religious system. "Well, you'll have anarchy." **Not** if you're **Spirit** controlled. If it's not Spirit bred, Spirit fed, and Spirit led, it's Babylon. The line's been drawn everywhere else—and Babylon took over **every** time—for **2,000** years! Let the plumb-bob drop.

Here's a warning clue (to leaders too—"a word to the wise" is—what? Snubbed? Ridiculed? Judged? Rejected? So be it.): if leaders live and lead, always uneasy (**out** spoken or **un** spoken) that people are going to be "led off" from **their** group (whatever the label) to become part of a different group, **be warned!** The leaders are Babylon-puffed and Jezebel-stuffed. They may not come right out and **tell** you they're uneasy. They could be too sly, or too deceived to know who they picked up "on the corner"—or they could just plain-out be too ambitious to give a hoot. They'll **lead you to believe** (one way or another, usually by cunning, "caring" ploys) that to leave **their** church, **their** denomination, **their**

group, **their** ministry, **their** whatever, means you'll lose your reward, if not your soul.

How much of this is going on? The how and the where is **shocking!** (How's the Spirit ever going to get all believers formed into one body by the Spirit without using moving-around body members?) Those poor "leaders" (Let's **pray** they're ignorant so there's mercy for them.) have **themselves** taken over for Holy Spirit. They **talk** unity and cooperation, and **do** nothing—maybe a token a year to keep their front shined up. Fear of members leaving **their** group, under **whatever** "shepherding" pretense used, is a sure symptom of Satan's system. I tell you, Babylon's Jezebel is on the prowl and wielding an uncanny, deadly control in church groups. Pick up on it. Preachers twist the "touch not my anointed" scripture, while messing over members like a drunk dragon. "Pretty gal's" got 'em with her spiritual "treats"—turning tricks right and left, waving "let's all work together" banners, and **spider-webbing you to a spot on the wall**. She's super sinister, a **dolled up** deadly "little darling thing"—primped by the evil pimp, sent straight out of hell to desensitize, organize, systematize and **"prettify"** the altars of God—set 'em up comfortable and beautiful under the shade. I couldn't improve on what the prophet said about her destiny: "**At last**, the oppressor is stilled; the whole earth is at rest and quiet. They break into song, **now that you are laid low**. Your pride has been brought down to Sh'ol with the music of your lyres, **under you a mattress of maggots, over you a blanket of worms**. I will cut off from

Bavel (Babylon) name and remnant, offshoot and offspring," says ADONAI. I will make it **a haunt for hedgehogs**, it will become **a swampy waste**, I will sweep it with the broom of destruction, says ADONAI-Tzva'ot." (See Isa 14 CJB) **Lord! Can I just be a bristle on this broom! Please! Please!**

Church
(Please note this: "We do not wrestle against flesh and blood, but against principalities, against powers, against the rulers of the darkness of this age, against spiritual *hosts* of wickedness in the heavenly *places.*" Eph 6:12 NKJV) When I seem to "attack the church," it is these "principalities, powers and rulers of the darkness of this age, and spiritual hosts of wickedness" that have **hidden out inside the church** that I'm going after—not the people, **not the people themselves**. I'm blasting to bring down the system that **holds** the people captive **so the people can go free.** I, myself, have served **long** prison terms in that jail and am bent on sparing a generation what I suffered. These chameleon like systems have turned the church into Babylon—it **was** headed for Jerusalem. Now, it's content with citizenship in "Christianized Babylon"—in all our brilliance, **we "fixed it up."**

Church, in reality, most times, is the "don't you dare question it" conglomerated religious hodge-podge, full of folk full of regimented thought patterns that **bar** them from the full presence of God. God's presence would **kill 'em** if they came any closer! They're not **equipped** to handle him. To call today's "church" a body of "called out believers," is not fair to readers, who for years have been staring at this **monster**, and wondering how we got so **stupid**. Do they want to join us? **Heavens no!** They run for their lives and I don't blame 'em. I don't want to be penned into tracking a treadmill in a **creativity-killer** either. "On the street," the word "church" is as meaningless now as the word "Christian"—tells people little or nothing, except, "Watch out!" Both words lie in the jargon-junk of religious clichés and charismatic buzzwords—no truth-force in 'em. This machine-driven thing, called generally "the church" is definitely **not** "the bride," so I don't pretend it is. Trapped and smothering somewhere inside this mix-mashed, many-sided system is part of the bride remnant, crying her heart out for the presence of God. **I want to help her out of there** by truth distinctions that free her.

Family of God—God as Father, Mother, Son (may include believers in earth and heaven).

Godhood—a synonym of Godhead, except Godhood may include all heavenly beings.

GodMates—the Wholeness of God that includes Father, Mother, Child—the God Family.

Jezebel spirit
 The "pride and joy" demon of the Babylon family. **Loves** to hang out with famous church "leaders." Makes its victims blinder than a cave bat,

having long ago convinced them it is the Holy Spirit helping them to build a platform to strut their spiritual stuff. **The victims** themselves **must** be the ones to say **where** you worship, **how** you worship, **who** you worship with, **where** you give money, **how much** money you give where, **where** you spend your life, **how** you spend your life, **with whom** you spend your life—are you **listening** to what you're reading? All that goes on under "shepherding clothing." If, if, **if** God's telling **them** to do all that stuff for me (**to** me is more accurate), **why do I need the Holy Spirit?** I can just pay them to do the spiritual stuff. **They** have the last word about it all—and they make jokes about how blind and stupid sheep are. These blinded brothers and sick sisters sleeping with Jezebel will have you tending their little scorpions and chameleons and raising pythons and dragons—**in "the church"**—wonderful, **safe** play pen for the whole snake den. Jezzy doesn't care what gender it clings with, but seems to me like it warps men worse, even though the woman Jezebel is its namesake. Maybe there are just more hotshot men preachers? Good old boys church club goes way on back. Shouldn't **somebody** tell these victims who's got 'em by the gizzard? Wouldn't **that** be love? God, his very own self, warned he would **kill her children** with death—**God** will kill them (unless he lied). I hate the mess (not the victims now). Is it not love to sound **Father's** warning **blast**? Victims are often "famous"—and deaf! Let's **all** just **quit** "doing the demon" at the Jezzy Ball!

Rapture

A present distraction about a future attraction—truth **twisted**, coiled up by religion-loving Satan to hinder the finalization of God's kingdom **here in earth.** God's working **so** hard to get his creation back from Satan. The church, ever since it got so smart as to leave its Jewish roots, has been waving its ("borrowed" from Jews) branches at heaven like a stranded stranger on a desert island with "Please, **please God**—come rapture me off to heaven so I won't have to **do** anything." God's trying to get us where we can **receive him** into earth **to change it**; the church keeps trying to give away escape tickets **out of** earth so the church won't have to take responsibility **for** changing it by her use of the power of her live-in God. We keep **colliding** with God "mid-air"—**not** good preparation for **meeting with** God **in** air in a future rapture. Paul was "raptured" (same Greek word), then "came back" to finish his part of the **kingdom on earth.** Did **Paul** do it wrong?

"Second Coming"

Connected one way or another with rapture. The Bible reveals **many** "comings" and "coming forths" of Christ. "Christ coming" is not just a once-come, twice-come, double shot. It's ongoing coming and coming forth—a regeneration **process.** "Final coming" would be more accurate scripturally.

Sophi—short for Sophia

Sophia

Wisdom. Transliteration of the Greek word usually translated wisdom. Used here to express God's femininity or God's female workings of the Holy Spirit.

YeShAbba

Yeshua-Abba-Spirit, merged into **one** word in an effort to better express God's wholeness in **one** word. "Trinity" seems cold, religious, impersonal to me. YeShAbba includes the actual **scriptural** words for God—Yeshua Son, Abba Father, and Spirit (**including** female and mother workings of God). So, **Ye** = Yeshua, **YeSh** = Yeshua (embracing Spirit), **Abba** = Father, **S** = Spirit—in the middle, embracing Son and Father, embraced **by** Son and Father— all one—YeShAbba. God is Spirit—**all** of God is Spirit. **Within** this one Spirit is working Father, Mother, and Child—all as one. God is family— lives, loves, and works as family. **YeShAbba**—a fresh expression for "Trinity." (Trinity is not in the Bible. The **components** of "YeShAbba" **are** there. It expresses this new-heaven, new-earth God-Creature formed when Jesus was glorified. It's easier than writing Yeshua-Abba-Spirit.)

Printed in the United States
1170300001B/1-24